This
Home Owner's Journal
Belongs To:

Name _____

Address _____

City, State, ZIP _____

Phone _____

QUICK REFERENCE PHONE NUMBERS

TYPE OF WORK	NAME	PHONE
Air Conditioner		
Carpenter		
Carpet Cleaner		
Drapery Cleaner		
Electrician		
General Handyperson		
Heating		
Lawn Maintenance		
Home Insurance		
Painter		
Paperer		
Plumber		
Sewer/Cesspool/Septic		
Other		

The
Home Owner's
Journal:

What I Did and
When I Did It

By Colleen Jenkins

Fourth Edition

BLUE SKY MARKETING INC.
PO Box 21583-S
St. Paul, MN 55121-1583 USA

The Home Owner's Journal:
What I Did and When I Did It

By Colleen Jenkins

Fourth Edition

Copyright © 1991, 1988, and 1987 by Colleen Jenkins
Copyright © 2000 by Blue Sky Marketing Inc.

Cover Design and Illustrations by Julia Schreifels

Printed in the United States of America

Published by:

BLUE SKY MARKETING INC.
PO Box 21583-S
St. Paul, MN 55121-1583 USA
(651) 456-5602
(800) 444-5450
www.HomeOwnersJournal.com

SAN 263-9394

ISBN 0-911493-25-5

56   55   54   53   52   51   50   49   48   47   46   45

TABLE OF CONTENTS

TABLE OF CONTENTS (continued)

THANK YOU ! ! !

At the request of the publisher, we *both* kept a running list of every person who contributed to this book. When the book was finally ready for press and we looked over the list, I was amazed that more than ninety people contributed! A big THANK YOU to all of you!

IMPORTANT PERSONAL PAPERS

List your important personal papers and where they are kept. Examples are your Will, life insurance policies, fire insurance policies, stocks and bonds. Also list the location of your safe deposit box and all bank accounts. Include policy limits and the name of your attorney, agents, and brokers, etc. Tell your emergency contact person(s) about this book and where it can be found.

Item	Details

HOW TO USE YOUR JOURNAL

This is the book I wish I had when we first bought our home forty years ago. I don't know how I managed without it. The fact is, I did not manage well at all. In all those years, I finally made the same mistake one too many times and decided to find a solution. I don't recall the precise instant, but it was either when I recently wallpapered the bathroom or when I painted the outside of the house.

The consequence of my failure to write down how much paint I used the last time was two gallons of custom mixed, non-returnable, paint (which is now considered hazardous waste) left over after I finished painting the house. Had I written down the amount I used the previous time, I would have saved myself time and money! When I estimated how often things like that probably happened in the more than forty years I have lived in my home, the need for this book became painfully clear. Believe me, I do NOT have money or time to waste.

I thought this book would be simple to do, but I actually wrote many drafts before arriving at what I think is a very practical, easy-to-use, and flexible journal. Since no two homes are alike, complete only the sections that are applicable to your home. (Don't forget to change the Table of Contents, too!) I suggest making all entries in pencil. This will allow you to easily make corrections and updates.

This book has 11 main chapters. The sections within each chapter are organized in alphabetical order, except where items have special relationships to each other.

Most main sections end with lined space for extra notes. These note segments can also be used as graph paper for drawings, etc. You may want to sketch the walls and show window and door measurements, wiring projects, or make notes about what to consider next time. Some sections are comprised of only a heading and lined paper for writing or drawing. This maximizes flexibility and enables you to tailor the section to fit your particular needs.

Good luck! Let me know what you think of the book & how we can improve it. As always, suggestions from readers were incorporated into this edition. Maybe yours will be in the next!

Colleen Jenkins, Author

PURCHASE, FINANCE, & INSURANCE

PURCHASE INFORMATION

Date We Moved In _____ Square Ft. of Home _____

Property Legal Description (block, lot no., etc.) _____

Lot Marker Locations _____

_____

_____

_____

Builder/Contractor's Company _____

    Contact Person _____ Phone _____

    Date Home Built (completed) _____

    Warranty on Construction _____

Land Development Company _____

    Contact Person _____ Phone _____

Real Estate Company _____

    Agent _____

    Office Phone _____ Cell Phone _____

Notes: _____

_____

FINANCE INFORMATION

Mortgage Company _____ Loan Officer _____

    Office Phone _____ Cell Phone _____

    Loan No. _____

    Loan Servicing Dept. Phone _____

New Mortgage Company (if your mortgage is sold) _____

    Loan No. _____

    Phone _____ Date Sold _____

    Mortgage Balance at Time of Sale _____

Notes: _____

_____

_____

Second Mortgage Company _____

Phone _____

Loan No. _____

Date _____

Balance of Principal on Original _____

Mortgage Information

Purchase Price _____ Price Asked _____

Downpayment _____ Appraised Value _____

Mortgage Amount _____ Location of Abstract _____

Mortgage Type (FHA, VA, Conventional, etc.) _____

Interest Rate (beginning, if adjustable*) _____

Terms (30 yr. fixed, adjustable*, etc.) _____

Points (no. & $ amount) _____

Realtor's Commission (% & $) _____

Other Closing Costs _____

Closing Date _____

*Adjustable Rate Mortgage (ARM) Information

Rate	Date of Change	Principal Remaining	Monthly P & I

Adjustment Interval _____

Index _____

Margin _____

Interest Rate Caps (yearly, lifetime, etc.) _____

_____

Monthly Payment Cap _____

Graduated Payments _____

Negative Amortization (y/n & limit) _____

"Introductory" Rate _____

Assumability _____

Convertibility _____

Prepayment Privilege _____

Points (including origination fee) _____

Other _____

INSURANCE INFORMATION

Title Insurance Company _____

Title Binder No. _____

Homeowner's Insurance Company _____

Agent's Name _____

Office Phone _____ Cell Phone _____

Policy No. _____

Expiration Date (Month & Day) _____

Notes: _____

_____

_____

_____

_____

_____

_____

_____

ATTIC

(Use tick marks at top & bottom to make graph paper)

BASEMENT

(Use tick marks at top & bottom to make graph paper)

BATHROOM NUMBER 1

FLOOR COVERING

Floor Measurements

Widest part of room from middle of doorway _____

Longest part of room from middle of doorway _____

Notes: _____

_____

Type & Material (nylon carpet, ceramic tile, etc.) _____

Purchased From _____ Date _____

Brand & Pattern _____

Color & No. _____ Warranty Period _____

Type of Backing _____ Pad Type _____

Cost/Unit $_____ No. of Units _____ Total $_____

Installed By _____ Attached With _____

Date _____ Cost $_____

Cleaned/Refinished By _____

Date 1 _____ Cost $_____

Date 2 _____ Cost $_____

Date 3 _____ Cost $_____

Notes: _____

_____

CEILING COVERING

Type of Covering (paint, spray texture, etc.) _____

Purchased From _____ Date _____

Brand & Pattern _____

Color & No. _____ Warranty Period _____

Applied with (texture roller, sprayer, etc.) _____

Cost/Unit $_____ No. of Units _____ Total $_____

Installed By _____

Date _____ Cost $_____

Notes: _____

_____

WINDOW COVERING

Window 1 Measurements

Height _____ Width _____ Top of Window to Floor _____ Trim Width _____

Type of Covering (draperies, blinds, etc.) _____

Purchased From _____ Cost $_____ Date _____

   Measurements of Window Covering _____

   Material & Cleaning Instructions _____

Cleaned By _____ Cost $_____ Date _____

Cleaned By _____ Cost $_____ Date _____

Notes: _____

_____

Window 2 Measurements

Height _____ Width _____ Top of Window to Floor _____ Trim Width _____

Type of Covering (draperies, blinds, etc.) _____

Purchased From _____ Cost $_____ Date _____

   Measurements of Window Covering _____

   Material & Cleaning Instructions _____

Cleaned By _____ Cost $_____ Date _____

Notes: _____

WALL COVERING

Wall Measurements

   North _____ South _____ East _____ West _____

Use "2nd Type of Covering" for woodwork or paneling. It has a "Refinished By" section.

1st Type of Covering (paint, paper, etc.) _____

Purchased From _____ Date _____

   Brand & Pattern _____

   Color & No. _____ Warranty Period _____

   Cost/Unit $_____ No. of Units _____ Total $_____

Installed By _____

   Date _____ Cost $_____

Notes: _____

_____

WALL COVERING (continued)

2nd **Type of Covering** (woodwork, paneling, etc.) _____

Purchased From _____ Date _____

    Brand & Pattern _____

    Color & No. _____ Warranty Period _____

    Cost/Unit $_____ No. of Units _____ Total $_____

Installed By _____

    Date _____ Cost $_____

Refinished By _____

    Date _____ Cost $_____

Notes: _____

_____

SAMPLES: PAINT, WALLPAPER, ETC.

attach swatch or paint daub here

FURNITURE/FIXTURES

Item	Purchased From	Date	Cost	Warranty

DOORS/TRIM

Purchased From _____ Date _____

    Brand & Style _____ Material (oak, steel, etc.)_____

    Stain/Paint Color & No. _____

      Finished With (polyurethane over stain, etc.) _____

Installed By _____ Total Cost $_____

Refinished By _____

    Refinished With _____

    Date _____ Cost $_____

Hardware Description _____

_____

    Purchased From _____ Date _____

    Cost/Unit $_____ No. of Units _____ Total $_____

Notes: _____

_____

EXTRA NOTES

(Use tick marks at top & bottom to make graph paper)

BATHROOM NUMBER 2

FLOOR COVERING

Floor Measurements

Widest part of room from middle of doorway _____

Longest part of room from middle of doorway _____

Notes: _____

_____

Type & Material (nylon carpet, ceramic tile, etc.) _____

Purchased From _____ Date _____

Brand & Pattern _____

Color & No. _____ Warranty Period _____

Type of Backing _____ Pad Type _____

Cost/Unit $_____ No. of Units _____ Total $_____

Installed By _____ Attached With _____

Date _____ Cost $_____

Cleaned/Refinished By _____

Date 1 _____ Cost $_____

Date 2 _____ Cost $_____

Date 3 _____ Cost $_____

Notes: _____

_____

CEILING COVERING

Type of Covering (paint, spray texture, etc.) _____

Purchased From _____ Date _____

Brand & Pattern _____

Color & No. _____ Warranty Period _____

Applied with (texture roller, sprayer, etc.) _____

Cost/Unit $_____ No. of Units _____ Total $_____

Installed By _____

Date _____ Cost $_____

Notes: _____

_____

18

WINDOW COVERING

Window 1 Measurements

Height _____ Width _____ Top of Window to Floor _____ Trim Width _____

Type of Covering (draperies, blinds, etc.) _____

Purchased From _____ Cost $_____ Date _____

   Measurements of Window Covering _____

   Material & Cleaning Instructions _____

Cleaned By _____ Cost $_____ Date _____

Cleaned By _____ Cost $_____ Date _____

Notes: _____

_____

Window 2 Measurements

Height _____ Width _____ Top of Window to Floor _____ Trim Width _____

Type of Covering (draperies, blinds, etc.) _____

Purchased From _____ Cost $_____ Date _____

   Measurements of Window Covering _____

   Material & Cleaning Instructions _____

Cleaned By _____ Cost $_____ Date _____

Notes: _____

WALL COVERING

Wall Measurements

   North _____ South _____ East _____ West _____

Use "2nd Type of Covering" for woodwork or paneling. It has a "Refinished By" section.

1st Type of Covering (paint, paper, etc.) _____

Purchased From _____ Date _____

   Brand & Pattern _____

   Color & No. _____ Warranty Period _____

   Cost/Unit $_____ No. of Units _____ Total $_____

Installed By _____

   Date _____ Cost $_____

Notes: _____

_____

WALL COVERING (continued)

2<u>nd</u> <u>**Type of Covering**</u> (woodwork, paneling, etc.) _____

Purchased From _____ Date _____

   Brand & Pattern _____

   Color & No. _____ Warranty Period _____

   Cost/Unit $_____ No. of Units _____ Total $_____

Installed By _____

   Date _____ Cost $_____

Refinished By _____

   Date _____ Cost $_____

Notes: _____

_____

SAMPLES: PAINT, WALLPAPER, ETC.

attach swatch or paint daub here

FURNITURE/FIXTURES

Item	Purchased From	Date	Cost	Warranty

DOORS/TRIM

Purchased From _____ Date _____

Brand & Style _____ Material (oak, steel, etc.)_____

Stain/Paint Color & No. _____

Finished With (polyurethane over stain, etc.) _____

Installed By _____ Total Cost $_____

Refinished By _____

Refinished With _____

Date _____ Cost $_____

Hardware Description _____

_____

Purchased From _____ Date _____

Cost/Unit $_____ No. of Units _____ Total $_____

Notes: _____

_____

EXTRA NOTES

(Use tick marks at top & bottom to make graph paper)

BATHROOM NUMBER 3

FLOOR COVERING

Floor Measurements

Widest part of room from middle of doorway _____

Longest part of room from middle of doorway _____

Notes: _____

_____

Type & Material (nylon carpet, ceramic tile, etc.) _____

Purchased From _____ Date _____

Brand & Pattern _____

Color & No. _____ Warranty Period _____

Type of Backing _____ Pad Type _____

Cost/Unit $_____ No. of Units _____ Total $_____

Installed By _____ Attached With _____

Date _____ Cost $_____

Cleaned/Refinished By _____

Date 1 _____ Cost $_____

Date 2 _____ Cost $_____

Date 3 _____ Cost $_____

Notes: _____

CEILING COVERING

Type of Covering (paint, spray texture, etc.) _____

Purchased From _____ Date _____

Brand & Pattern _____

Color & No. _____ Warranty Period _____

Applied with (texture roller, sprayer, etc.) _____

Cost/Unit $_____ No. of Units _____ Total $_____

Installed By _____

Date _____ Cost $_____

Notes: _____

_____

WINDOW COVERING

Window 1 Measurements

Height _____ Width _____ Top of Window to Floor _____ Trim Width _____

Type of Covering (draperies, blinds, etc.) _____

Purchased From _____ Cost $_____ Date _____

   Measurements of Window Covering _____

   Material & Cleaning Instructions _____

Cleaned By _____ Cost $_____ Date _____

Cleaned By _____ Cost $_____ Date _____

Notes: _____

_____

Window 2 Measurements

Height _____ Width _____ Top of Window to Floor _____ Trim Width _____

Type of Covering (draperies, blinds, etc.) _____

Purchased From _____ Cost $_____ Date _____

   Measurements of Window Covering _____

   Material & Cleaning Instructions _____

Cleaned By _____ Cost $_____ Date _____

Notes: _____

WALL COVERING

Wall Measurements

   North _____ South _____ East _____ West _____

Use "2nd Type of Covering" for woodwork or paneling. It has a "Refinished By" section.

1st Type of Covering (paint, paper, etc.) _____

Purchased From _____ Date _____

   Brand & Pattern _____

   Color & No. _____ Warranty Period _____

   Cost/Unit $_____ No. of Units _____ Total $_____

Installed By _____

   Date _____ Cost $_____

Notes: _____

_____

23

WALL COVERING (continued)

<u>**2nd Type of Covering**</u> (woodwork, paneling, etc.) _____

Purchased From _____ Date _____

   Brand & Pattern _____

   Color & No. _____ Warranty Period _____

   Cost/Unit $_____ No. of Units _____ Total $_____

Installed By _____

   Date _____ Cost $_____

Refinished By _____

   Date _____ Cost $_____

Notes: _____

_____

SAMPLES: PAINT, WALLPAPER, ETC.

attach swatch or paint daub here

FURNITURE/FIXTURES

Item	Purchased From	Date	Cost	Warranty

DOORS/TRIM

Purchased From _____ Date _____

    Brand & Style _____ Material (oak, steel, etc.)_____

    Stain/Paint Color & No. _____

      Finished With (polyurethane over stain, etc.) _____

Installed By _____ Total Cost $_____

Refinished By _____

    Refinished With _____

    Date _____ Cost $_____

Hardware Description _____

_____

    Purchased From _____ Date _____

    Cost/Unit $_____ No. of Units _____ Total $_____

Notes: _____

_____

EXTRA NOTES

(Use tick marks at top & bottom to make graph paper)

BEDROOM NUMBER 1

FLOOR COVERING

Floor Measurements

Widest part of room from middle of doorway _____

Longest part of room from middle of doorway _____

Notes: _____

_____

Type & Material (nylon carpet, ceramic tile, etc.) _____

Purchased From _____ Date _____

Brand & Pattern _____

Color & No. _____ Warranty Period _____

Type of Backing _____ Pad Type _____

Cost/Unit $_____ No. of Units _____ Total $_____

Installed By _____ Attached With _____

Date _____ Cost $_____

Cleaned/Refinished By _____

Date 1 _____ Cost $_____

Date 2 _____ Cost $_____

Date 3 _____ Cost $_____

Notes: _____

_____

CEILING COVERING

Type of Covering (paint, spray texture, etc.) _____

Purchased From _____ Date _____

Brand & Pattern _____

Color & No. _____ Warranty Period _____

Applied with (texture roller, sprayer, etc.) _____

Cost/Unit $_____ No. of Units _____ Total $_____

Installed By _____

Date _____ Cost $_____

Notes: _____

_____

WINDOW COVERING

Window 1 Measurements

Height _____ Width _____ Top of Window to Floor _____ Trim Width _____

Type of Covering (draperies, blinds, etc.) _____

Purchased From _____ Cost $_____ Date _____

   Measurements of Window Covering _____

   Material & Cleaning Instructions _____

Cleaned By _____ Cost $_____ Date _____

Cleaned By _____ Cost $_____ Date _____

Notes: _____

_____

_____

Window 2 Measurements

Height _____ Width _____ Top of Window to Floor _____ Trim Width _____

Type of Covering (draperies, blinds, etc.) _____

Purchased From _____ Cost $_____ Date _____

   Measurements of Window Covering _____

   Material & Cleaning Instructions _____

Cleaned By _____ Cost $_____ Date _____

Notes: _____

_____

Window 3 Measurements

Height _____ Width _____ Top of Window to Floor _____ Trim Width _____

Type of Covering (draperies, blinds, etc.) _____

Purchased From _____ Cost $_____ Date _____

   Measurements of Window Covering _____

   Material & Cleaning Instructions _____

Cleaned By _____ Cost $_____ Date _____

Notes: _____

_____

WALL COVERING

Wall Measurements

North _____ South _____ East _____ West _____

Use "2nd Type of Covering" for woodwork or paneling. It has a "Refinished By" section.

1st Type of Covering (paint, paper, etc.) _____

Purchased From _____ Date _____

Brand & Pattern _____

Color & No. _____ Warranty Period _____

Cost/Unit $_____ No. of Units _____ Total $_____

Installed By _____

Date _____ Cost $_____

Notes: _____

_____

2nd Type of Covering (paint, paper, etc.) _____

Purchased From _____ Date _____

Brand & Pattern _____

Color & No. _____ Warranty Period _____

Cost/Unit $_____ No. of Units _____ Total $_____

Installed By _____

Date _____ Cost $_____

Refinished By _____

Date _____ Cost $_____

Notes: _____

_____

SAMPLES: PAINT, WALLPAPER, ETC.

attach swatch or paint daub here

DOORS/TRIM

Purchased From _____ Date _____

   Brand & Style _____ Material (oak, steel, etc.)_____

   Stain/Paint Color & No. _____

    Finished With (polyurethane over stain, etc.) _____

Installed By _____ Total Cost $_____

Refinished By _____

   Refinished With _____

   Date _____ Cost $_____

Hardware Description _____

_____

   Purchased From _____ Date _____

   Cost/Unit $_____ No. of Units _____ Total $_____

Notes: _____

_____

FURNITURE/FIXTURES

Item	Purchased From	Date	Cost	Warranty

EXTRA NOTES
(Use tick marks at top & bottom to make graph paper)

BEDROOM NUMBER 2

FLOOR COVERING

Floor Measurements

Widest part of room from middle of doorway _____

Longest part of room from middle of doorway _____

Notes: _____

_____

Type & Material (nylon carpet, ceramic tile, etc.) _____

Purchased From _____ Date _____

Brand & Pattern _____

Color & No. _____ Warranty Period _____

Type of Backing _____ Pad Type _____

Cost/Unit $_____ No. of Units _____ Total $_____

Installed By _____ Attached With _____

Date _____ Cost $_____

Cleaned/Refinished By _____

Date 1 _____ Cost $_____

Date 2 _____ Cost $_____

Date 3 _____ Cost $_____

Notes: _____

_____

CEILING COVERING

Type of Covering (paint, spray texture, etc.) _____

Purchased From _____ Date _____

Brand & Pattern _____

Color & No. _____ Warranty Period _____

Applied with (texture roller, sprayer, etc.) _____

Cost/Unit $_____ No. of Units _____ Total $_____

Installed By _____

Date _____ Cost $_____

Notes: _____

_____

WINDOW COVERING

Window 1 Measurements

Height _____ Width _____ Top of Window to Floor _____ Trim Width _____

Type of Covering (draperies, blinds, etc.) _____

Purchased From _____ Cost $_____ Date _____

   Measurements of Window Covering _____

   Material & Cleaning Instructions _____

Cleaned By _____ Cost $_____ Date _____

Cleaned By _____ Cost $_____ Date _____

Notes: _____

_____

_____

Window 2 Measurements

Height _____ Width _____ Top of Window to Floor _____ Trim Width _____

Type of Covering (draperies, blinds, etc.) _____

Purchased From _____ Cost $_____ Date _____

   Measurements of Window Covering _____

   Material & Cleaning Instructions _____

Cleaned By _____ Cost $_____ Date _____

Notes: _____

_____

Window 3 Measurements

Height _____ Width _____ Top of Window to Floor _____ Trim Width _____

Type of Covering (draperies, blinds, etc.) _____

Purchased From _____ Cost $_____ Date _____

   Measurements of Window Covering _____

   Material & Cleaning Instructions _____

Cleaned By _____ Cost $_____ Date _____

Notes: _____

_____

WALL COVERING

<u>Wall Measurements</u>

North _____ South _____ East _____ West _____

Use "2nd Type of Covering" for woodwork or paneling. It has a "Refinished By" section.

1ˢᵗ Type of Covering (paint, paper, etc.) _____

Purchased From _____ Date _____

    Brand & Pattern _____

    Color & No. _____ Warranty Period _____

    Cost/Unit $_____ No. of Units _____ Total $_____

Installed By _____

    Date _____ Cost $_____

Notes: _____

_____

2ⁿᵈ Type of Covering (paint, paper, etc.) _____

Purchased From _____ Date _____

    Brand & Pattern _____

    Color & No. _____ Warranty Period _____

    Cost/Unit $_____ No. of Units _____ Total $_____

Installed By _____

    Date _____ Cost $_____

Refinished By _____

    Date _____ Cost $_____

Notes: _____

_____

SAMPLES: PAINT, WALLPAPER, ETC.

attach swatch or paint daub here

DOORS/TRIM

Purchased From _____ Date _____

    Brand & Style _____ Material (oak, steel, etc.)_____

    Stain/Paint Color & No. _____

    Finished With (polyurethane over stain, etc.) _____

Installed By _____ Total Cost $_____

Refinished By _____

    Refinished With _____

    Date _____ Cost $_____

Hardware Description _____

_____

    Purchased From _____ Date _____

    Cost/Unit $_____ No. of Units _____ Total $_____

Notes: _____

FURNITURE/FIXTURES

Item	Purchased From	Date	Cost	Warranty

EXTRA NOTES

(Use tick marks at top & bottom to make graph paper)

33

BEDROOM NUMBER 3

FLOOR COVERING

Floor Measurements

Widest part of room from middle of doorway _____

Longest part of room from middle of doorway _____

Notes: _____

_____

Type & Material (nylon carpet, ceramic tile, etc.) _____

Purchased From _____ Date _____

Brand & Pattern _____

Color & No. _____ Warranty Period _____

Type of Backing _____ Pad Type _____

Cost/Unit $_____ No. of Units _____ Total $_____

Installed By _____ Attached With _____

Date _____ Cost $_____

Cleaned/Refinished By _____

Date 1 _____ Cost $_____

Date 2 _____ Cost $_____

Date 3 _____ Cost $_____

Notes: _____

_____

CEILING COVERING

Type of Covering (paint, spray texture, etc.) _____

Purchased From _____ Date _____

Brand & Pattern _____

Color & No. _____ Warranty Period _____

Applied with (texture roller, sprayer, etc.) _____

Cost/Unit $_____ No. of Units _____ Total $_____

Installed By _____

Date _____ Cost $_____

Notes: _____

_____

34

WINDOW COVERING

Window 1 Measurements

Height _____ Width _____ Top of Window to Floor _____ Trim Width _____

Type of Covering (draperies, blinds, etc.) _____

Purchased From _____ Cost $_____ Date _____

   Measurements of Window Covering _____

   Material & Cleaning Instructions _____

Cleaned By _____ Cost $_____ Date _____

Cleaned By _____ Cost $_____ Date _____

Notes: _____

_____

_____

Window 2 Measurements

Height _____ Width _____ Top of Window to Floor _____ Trim Width _____

Type of Covering (draperies, blinds, etc.) _____

Purchased From _____ Cost $_____ Date _____

   Measurements of Window Covering _____

   Material & Cleaning Instructions _____

Cleaned By _____ Cost $_____ Date _____

Notes: _____

_____

Window 3 Measurements

Height _____ Width _____ Top of Window to Floor _____ Trim Width _____

Type of Covering (draperies, blinds, etc.) _____

Purchased From _____ Cost $_____ Date _____

   Measurements of Window Covering _____

   Material & Cleaning Instructions _____

Cleaned By _____ Cost $_____ Date _____

Notes: _____

_____

WALL COVERING

Wall Measurements

North _____ South _____ East _____ West _____

Use "2nd Type of Covering" for woodwork or paneling. It has a "Refinished By" section.

1st Type of Covering (paint, paper, etc.) _____

Purchased From _____ Date _____

Brand & Pattern _____

Color & No. _____ Warranty Period _____

Cost/Unit $_____ No. of Units _____ Total $_____

Installed By _____

Date _____ Cost $_____

Notes: _____

_____

2nd Type of Covering (paint, paper, etc.) _____

Purchased From _____ Date _____

Brand & Pattern _____

Color & No. _____ Warranty Period _____

Cost/Unit $_____ No. of Units _____ Total $_____

Installed By _____

Date _____ Cost $_____

Refinished By _____

Date _____ Cost $_____

Notes: _____

_____

SAMPLES: PAINT, WALLPAPER, ETC.

attach swatch or paint daub here

DOORS/TRIM

Purchased From _____ Date _____

    Brand & Style _____ Material (oak, steel, etc.)_____

    Stain/Paint Color & No. _____

      Finished With (polyurethane over stain, etc.) _____

Installed By _____ Total Cost $_____

Refinished By _____

    Refinished With _____

    Date _____ Cost $_____

Hardware Description _____

_____

    Purchased From _____ Date _____

    Cost/Unit $_____ No. of Units _____ Total $_____

Notes: _____

_____

FURNITURE/FIXTURES

Item	Purchased From	Date	Cost	Warranty

EXTRA NOTES
(Use tick marks at top & bottom to make graph paper)

37

BEDROOM NUMBER 4

FLOOR COVERING

Floor Measurements

Widest part of room from middle of doorway _____

Longest part of room from middle of doorway _____

Notes: _____

_____

Type & Material (nylon carpet, ceramic tile, etc.) _____

Purchased From _____ Date _____

Brand & Pattern _____

Color & No. _____ Warranty Period _____

Type of Backing _____ Pad Type _____

Cost/Unit $_____ No. of Units _____ Total $_____

Installed By _____ Attached With _____

Date _____ Cost $_____

Cleaned/Refinished By _____

Date 1 _____ Cost $_____

Date 2 _____ Cost $_____

Date 3 _____ Cost $_____

Notes: _____

_____

CEILING COVERING

Type of Covering (paint, spray texture, etc.) _____

Purchased From _____ Date _____

Brand & Pattern _____

Color & No. _____ Warranty Period _____

Applied with (texture roller, sprayer, etc.) _____

Cost/Unit $_____ No. of Units _____ Total $_____

Installed By _____

Date _____ Cost $_____

Notes: _____

_____

38

BEDROOM NUMBER 4 (continued)

WINDOW COVERING

Window 1 Measurements

Height _____ Width _____ Top of Window to Floor _____ Trim Width _____

Type of Covering (draperies, blinds, etc.) _____

Purchased From _____ Cost $_____ Date _____

   Measurements of Window Covering _____

   Material & Cleaning Instructions _____

Cleaned By _____ Cost $_____ Date _____

Cleaned By _____ Cost $_____ Date _____

Notes: _____

_____

_____

Window 2 Measurements

Height _____ Width _____ Top of Window to Floor _____ Trim Width _____

Type of Covering (draperies, blinds, etc.) _____

Purchased From _____ Cost $_____ Date _____

   Measurements of Window Covering _____

   Material & Cleaning Instructions _____

Cleaned By _____ Cost $_____ Date _____

Notes: _____

_____

Window 3 Measurements

Height _____ Width _____ Top of Window to Floor _____ Trim Width _____

Type of Covering (draperies, blinds, etc.) _____

Purchased From _____ Cost $_____ Date _____

   Measurements of Window Covering _____

   Material & Cleaning Instructions _____

Cleaned By _____ Cost $_____ Date _____

Notes: _____

_____

WALL COVERING

<u>**Wall Measurements**</u>

North _____ South _____ East _____ West _____

Use "2nd Type of Covering" for woodwork or paneling. It has a "Refinished By" section.

1ˢᵗ Type of Covering (paint, paper, etc.) _____

Purchased From _____ Date _____

    Brand & Pattern _____

    Color & No. _____ Warranty Period _____

    Cost/Unit $_____ No. of Units _____ Total $_____

Installed By _____

    Date _____ Cost $_____

Notes: _____

_____

2ⁿᵈ Type of Covering (paint, paper, etc.) _____

Purchased From _____ Date _____

    Brand & Pattern _____

    Color & No. _____ Warranty Period _____

    Cost/Unit $_____ No. of Units _____ Total $_____

Installed By _____

    Date _____ Cost $_____

Refinished By _____

    Date _____ Cost $_____

Notes: _____

_____

SAMPLES: PAINT, WALLPAPER, ETC.

attach swatch or paint daub here

DOORS/TRIM

Purchased From _____ Date _____

   Brand & Style _____ Material (oak, steel, etc.)_____

   Stain/Paint Color & No. _____

     Finished With (polyurethane over stain, etc.) _____

Installed By _____ Total Cost $_____

Refinished By _____

   Refinished With _____

   Date _____ Cost $_____

Hardware Description _____

_____

   Purchased From _____ Date _____

   Cost/Unit $_____ No. of Units _____ Total $_____

Notes: _____

_____

FURNITURE/FIXTURES

Item	Purchased From	Date	Cost	Warranty

EXTRA NOTES
(Use tick marks at top & bottom to make graph paper)

DEN/STUDY/OFFICE
FLOOR COVERING

Floor Measurements

Widest part of room from middle of doorway _____

Longest part of room from middle of doorway _____

Notes: _____

_____

Type & Material (nylon carpet, ceramic tile, etc.) _____

Purchased From _____ Date _____

Brand & Pattern _____

Color & No. _____ Warranty Period _____

Type of Backing _____ Pad Type _____

Cost/Unit $_____ No. of Units _____ Total $_____

Installed By _____ Attached With _____

Date _____ Cost $_____

Cleaned/Refinished By _____

Date 1 _____ Cost $_____

Date 2 _____ Cost $_____

Date 3 _____ Cost $_____

Notes: _____

_____

CEILING COVERING

Type of Covering (paint, spray texture, etc.) _____

Purchased From _____ Date _____

Brand & Pattern _____

Color & No. _____ Warranty Period _____

Applied with (texture roller, sprayer, etc.) _____

Cost/Unit $_____ No. of Units _____ Total $_____

Installed By _____

Date _____ Cost $_____

Notes: _____

_____

WINDOW COVERING

Window 1 Measurements

Height _____ Width _____ Top of Window to Floor _____ Trim Width _____

Type of Covering (draperies, blinds, etc.) _____

Purchased From _____ Cost $_____ Date _____

   Measurements of Window Covering _____

   Material & Cleaning Instructions _____

Cleaned By _____ Cost $_____ Date _____

Cleaned By _____ Cost $_____ Date _____

Notes: _____

_____

_____

Window 2 Measurements

Height _____ Width _____ Top of Window to Floor _____ Trim Width _____

Type of Covering (draperies, blinds, etc.) _____

Purchased From _____ Cost $_____ Date _____

   Measurements of Window Covering _____

   Material & Cleaning Instructions _____

Cleaned By _____ Cost $_____ Date _____

Notes: _____

_____

Window 3 Measurements

Height _____ Width _____ Top of Window to Floor _____ Trim Width _____

Type of Covering (draperies, blinds, etc.) _____

Purchased From _____ Cost $_____ Date _____

   Measurements of Window Covering _____

   Material & Cleaning Instructions _____

Cleaned By _____ Cost $_____ Date _____

Notes: _____

_____

WALL COVERING

Wall Measurements

North _____ South _____ East _____ West _____

Use "2nd Type of Covering" for woodwork or paneling. It has a "Refinished By" section.

1st Type of Covering (paint, paper, etc.) _____

Purchased From _____ Date _____

   Brand & Pattern _____

   Color & No. _____ Warranty Period _____

   Cost/Unit $_____ No. of Units _____ Total $_____

Installed By _____

   Date _____ Cost $_____

Notes: _____

_____

2nd Type of Covering (paint, paper, etc.) _____

Purchased From _____ Date _____

   Brand & Pattern _____

   Color & No. _____ Warranty Period _____

   Cost/Unit $_____ No. of Units _____ Total $_____

Installed By _____

   Date _____ Cost $_____

Refinished By _____

   Date _____ Cost $_____

Notes: _____

_____

SAMPLES: PAINT, WALLPAPER, ETC.

attach swatch or paint daub here

44

DOORS/TRIM

Purchased From _____ Date _____

  Brand & Style _____ Material (oak, steel, etc.)_____

  Stain/Paint Color & No. _____

    Finished With (polyurethane over stain, etc.) _____

Installed By _____ Total Cost $_____

Refinished By _____

  Refinished With _____

  Date _____ Cost $_____

Hardware Description _____

_____

  Purchased From _____ Date _____

  Cost/Unit $_____ No. of Units _____ Total $_____

Notes: _____

_____

FURNITURE/FIXTURES

Item	Purchased From	Date	Cost	Warranty

EXTRA NOTES

(Use tick marks at top & bottom to make graph paper)

DINING ROOM

FLOOR COVERING

Floor Measurements

Widest part of room from middle of doorway _____

Longest part of room from middle of doorway _____

Notes: _____

_____

Type & Material (nylon carpet, ceramic tile, etc.) _____

Purchased From _____ Date _____

Brand & Pattern _____

Color & No. _____ Warranty Period _____

Type of Backing _____ Pad Type _____

Cost/Unit $_____ No. of Units _____ Total $_____

Installed By _____ Attached With _____

Date _____ Cost $_____

Cleaned/Refinished By _____

Date 1 _____ Cost $_____

Date 2 _____ Cost $_____

Date 3 _____ Cost $_____

Notes: _____

_____

CEILING COVERING

Type of Covering (paint, spray texture, etc.) _____

Purchased From _____ Date _____

Brand & Pattern _____

Color & No. _____ Warranty Period _____

Applied with (texture roller, sprayer, etc.) _____

Cost/Unit $_____ No. of Units _____ Total $_____

Installed By _____

Date _____ Cost $_____

Notes: _____

_____

WINDOW COVERING

Window 1 Measurements

Height _____ Width _____ Top of Window to Floor _____ Trim Width _____

Type of Covering (draperies, blinds, etc.) _____

Purchased From _____ Cost $_____ Date _____

   Measurements of Window Covering _____

   Material & Cleaning Instructions _____

Cleaned By _____ Cost $_____ Date _____

Cleaned By _____ Cost $_____ Date _____

Notes: _____

_____

_____

Window 2 Measurements

Height _____ Width _____ Top of Window to Floor _____ Trim Width _____

Type of Covering (draperies, blinds, etc.) _____

Purchased From _____ Cost $_____ Date _____

   Measurements of Window Covering _____

   Material & Cleaning Instructions _____

Cleaned By _____ Cost $_____ Date _____

Notes: _____

_____

Window 3 Measurements

Height _____ Width _____ Top of Window to Floor _____ Trim Width _____

Type of Covering (draperies, blinds, etc.) _____

Purchased From _____ Cost $_____ Date _____

   Measurements of Window Covering _____

   Material & Cleaning Instructions _____

Cleaned By _____ Cost $_____ Date _____

Notes: _____

_____

WALL COVERING

Wall Measurements

North _____ South _____ East _____ West _____

Use "2nd Type of Covering" for woodwork or paneling. It has a "Refinished By" section.

1st Type of Covering (paint, paper, etc.) _____

Purchased From _____ Date _____

    Brand & Pattern _____

    Color & No. _____ Warranty Period _____

    Cost/Unit $_____ No. of Units _____ Total $_____

Installed By _____

    Date _____ Cost $_____

Notes: _____

_____

2nd Type of Covering (paint, paper, etc.) _____

Purchased From _____ Date _____

    Brand & Pattern _____

    Color & No. _____ Warranty Period _____

    Cost/Unit $_____ No. of Units _____ Total $_____

Installed By _____

    Date _____ Cost $_____

Refinished By _____

    Date _____ Cost $_____

Notes: _____

_____

SAMPLES: PAINT, WALLPAPER, ETC.

attach swatch or paint daub here

DOORS/TRIM

Purchased From _____ Date _____

   Brand & Style _____ Material (oak, steel, etc.)_____

   Stain/Paint Color & No. _____

     Finished With (polyurethane over stain, etc.) _____

Installed By _____ Total Cost $_____

Refinished By _____

   Refinished With _____

   Date _____ Cost $_____

Hardware Description _____

_____

   Purchased From _____ Date _____

   Cost/Unit $_____ No. of Units _____ Total $_____

Notes: _____

_____

FURNITURE/FIXTURES

Item	Purchased From	Date	Cost	Warranty

EXTRA NOTES

(Use tick marks at top & bottom to make graph paper)

ELECTRICAL/WIRING

(Suggestion: Use tick marks at top & bottom to make graph paper. Sketch the layout of your circuit/fuse box. Label the circuits/fuses and identify the outlets and appliances they control.)

ENTRY/FOYER/MUD ROOM

FLOOR COVERING

Floor Measurements

Widest part of room from middle of doorway _____

Longest part of room from middle of doorway _____

Notes: _____

_____

Type & Material (nylon carpet, ceramic tile, etc.) _____

Purchased From _____ Date _____

Brand & Pattern _____

Color & No. _____ Warranty Period _____

Type of Backing _____ Pad Type _____

Cost/Unit $_____ No. of Units _____ Total $_____

Installed By _____ Attached With _____

Date _____ Cost $_____

Cleaned/Refinished By _____

Date 1 _____ Cost $_____

Date 2 _____ Cost $_____

Date 3 _____ Cost $_____

Notes: _____

_____

CEILING COVERING

Type of Covering (paint, spray texture, etc.) _____

Purchased From _____ Date _____

Brand & Pattern _____

Color & No. _____ Warranty Period _____

Applied with (texture roller, sprayer, etc.) _____

Cost/Unit $_____ No. of Units _____ Total $_____

Installed By _____

Date _____ Cost $_____

Notes: _____

_____

WINDOW COVERING

Window 1 Measurements

Height _____ Width _____ Top of Window to Floor _____ Trim Width _____

Type of Covering (draperies, blinds, etc.) _____

Purchased From _____ Cost $_____ Date _____

    Measurements of Window Covering _____

    Material & Cleaning Instructions _____

Cleaned By _____ Cost $_____ Date _____

Cleaned By _____ Cost $_____ Date _____

Notes: _____

WALL COVERING

Wall Measurements

    North _____ South _____ East _____ West _____

    Use "2nd Type of Covering" for woodwork or paneling. It has a "Refinished By" section.

1st Type of Covering (paint, paper, etc.) _____

Purchased From _____ Date _____

    Brand & Pattern _____

    Color & No. _____ Warranty Period _____

    Cost/Unit $_____ No. of Units _____ Total $_____

Installed By _____

    Date _____ Cost $_____

Notes: _____

2nd Type of Covering (paint, paper, etc.) _____

Purchased From _____ Date _____

    Brand & Pattern _____

    Color & No. _____ Warranty Period _____

    Cost/Unit $_____ No. of Units _____ Total $_____

Installed By _____

    Date _____ Cost $_____

Refinished By _____

    Date _____ Cost $_____

Notes: _____

SAMPLES: PAINT, WALLPAPER, ETC.

attach swatch or paint daub here

DOORS/TRIM

Purchased From _____ Date _____

    Brand & Style _____ Material (oak, steel, etc.)_____

    Stain/Paint Color & No. _____

      Finished With (polyurethane over stain, etc.) _____

Installed By _____ Total Cost $_____

Refinished By _____

    Refinished With _____

    Date _____ Cost $_____

Hardware Description _____

    Purchased From _____ Date _____

    Cost/Unit $_____ No. of Units _____ Total $_____

Notes: _____

FURNITURE/FIXTURES

Item	Purchased From	Date	Cost	Warranty

EXTRA NOTES

_____

_____

_____

_____

FAMILY ROOM

FLOOR COVERING

Floor Measurements

Widest part of room from middle of doorway _____

Longest part of room from middle of doorway _____

Notes: _____

_____

Type & Material (nylon carpet, ceramic tile, etc.) _____

Purchased From _____ Date _____

Brand & Pattern _____

Color & No. _____ Warranty Period _____

Type of Backing _____ Pad Type _____

Cost/Unit $_____ No. of Units _____ Total $_____

Installed By _____ Attached With _____

Date _____ Cost $_____

Cleaned/Refinished By _____

Date 1 _____ Cost $_____

Date 2 _____ Cost $_____

Date 3 _____ Cost $_____

Notes: _____

_____

CEILING COVERING

Type of Covering (paint, spray texture, etc.) _____

Purchased From _____ Date _____

Brand & Pattern _____

Color & No. _____ Warranty Period _____

Applied with (texture roller, sprayer, etc.) _____

Cost/Unit $_____ No. of Units _____ Total $_____

Installed By _____

Date _____ Cost $_____

Notes: _____

_____

WINDOW COVERING

Window 1 Measurements

Height _____ Width _____ Top of Window to Floor _____ Trim Width _____

Type of Covering (draperies, blinds, etc.) _____

Purchased From _____ Cost $_____ Date _____

    Measurements of Window Covering _____

    Material & Cleaning Instructions _____

Cleaned By _____ Cost $_____ Date _____

Cleaned By _____ Cost $_____ Date _____

Notes: _____

_____

_____

Window 2 Measurements

Height _____ Width _____ Top of Window to Floor _____ Trim Width _____

Type of Covering (draperies, blinds, etc.) _____

Purchased From _____ Cost $_____ Date _____

    Measurements of Window Covering _____

    Material & Cleaning Instructions _____

Cleaned By _____ Cost $_____ Date _____

Notes: _____

_____

Window 3 Measurements

Height _____ Width _____ Top of Window to Floor _____ Trim Width _____

Type of Covering (draperies, blinds, etc.) _____

Purchased From _____ Cost $_____ Date _____

    Measurements of Window Covering _____

    Material & Cleaning Instructions _____

Cleaned By _____ Cost $_____ Date _____

Notes: _____

_____

WALL COVERING

Wall Measurements

North _____ South _____ East _____ West _____

Use "2nd Type of Covering" for woodwork or paneling. It has a "Refinished By" section.

1st Type of Covering (paint, paper, etc.) _____

Purchased From _____ Date _____

    Brand & Pattern _____

    Color & No. _____ Warranty Period _____

    Cost/Unit $_____ No. of Units _____ Total $_____

Installed By _____

    Date _____ Cost $_____

Notes: _____

_____

2nd Type of Covering (paint, paper, etc.) _____

Purchased From _____ Date _____

    Brand & Pattern _____

    Color & No. _____ Warranty Period _____

    Cost/Unit $_____ No. of Units _____ Total $_____

Installed By _____

    Date _____ Cost $_____

Refinished By _____

    Date _____ Cost $_____

Notes: _____

_____

SAMPLES: PAINT, WALLPAPER, ETC.

attach swatch or paint daub here

DOORS/TRIM

Purchased From _____ Date _____

    Brand & Style _____ Material (oak, steel, etc.)_____

    Stain/Paint Color & No. _____

    Finished With (polyurethane over stain, etc.) _____

Installed By _____ Total Cost $_____

Refinished By _____

    Refinished With _____

    Date _____ Cost $_____

Hardware Description _____

_____

    Purchased From _____ Date _____

    Cost/Unit $_____ No. of Units _____ Total $_____

Notes: _____

_____

FURNITURE/FIXTURES

Item	Purchased From	Date	Cost	Warranty

EXTRA NOTES

(Use tick marks at top & bottom to make graph paper)

HALLWAY/STAIRWAY I

FLOOR COVERING

Floor Measurements

Widest part of room from middle of doorway _____

Longest part of room from middle of doorway _____

Notes: _____

_____

Type & Material (nylon carpet, ceramic tile, etc.) _____

Purchased From _____ Date _____

Brand & Pattern _____

Color & No. _____ Warranty Period _____

Type of Backing _____ Pad Type _____

Cost/Unit $_____ No. of Units _____ Total $_____

Installed By _____ Attached With _____

Date _____ Cost $_____

Cleaned/Refinished By _____

Date 1 _____ Cost $_____

Date 2 _____ Cost $_____

Date 3 _____ Cost $_____

Notes: _____

_____

CEILING COVERING

Type of Covering (paint, spray texture, etc.) _____

Purchased From _____ Date _____

Brand & Pattern _____

Color & No. _____ Warranty Period _____

Applied with (texture roller, sprayer, etc.) _____

Cost/Unit $_____ No. of Units _____ Total $_____

Installed By _____

Date _____ Cost $_____

Notes: _____

_____

WINDOW COVERING

Window 1 Measurements

Height _____ Width _____ Top of Window to Floor _____ Trim Width _____

Type of Covering (draperies, blinds, etc.) _____

Purchased From _____ Cost $_____ Date _____

    Measurements of Window Covering _____

    Material & Cleaning Instructions _____

Cleaned By _____ Cost $_____ Date _____

Cleaned By _____ Cost $_____ Date _____

Notes: _____

WALL COVERING

Wall Measurements

    North _____ South _____ East _____ West _____

Use "2nd Type of Covering" for woodwork or paneling. It has a "Refinished By" section.

1st Type of Covering (paint, paper, etc.) _____

Purchased From _____ Date _____

    Brand & Pattern _____

    Color & No. _____ Warranty Period _____

    Cost/Unit $_____ No. of Units _____ Total $_____

Installed By _____

    Date _____ Cost $_____

Notes: _____

2nd Type of Covering (paint, paper, etc.) _____

Purchased From _____ Date _____

    Brand & Pattern _____

    Color & No. _____ Warranty Period _____

    Cost/Unit $_____ No. of Units _____ Total $_____

Installed By _____

    Date _____ Cost $_____

Refinished By _____

    Date _____ Cost $_____

Notes: _____

SAMPLES: PAINT, WALLPAPER, ETC.

attach swatch or paint daub here

DOORS/TRIM

Purchased From _____ Date _____

   Brand & Style _____ Material (oak, steel, etc.)_____

   Stain/Paint Color & No. _____

    Finished With (polyurethane over stain, etc.) _____

Installed By _____ Total Cost $_____

Refinished By _____

   Refinished With _____

   Date _____ Cost $_____

Hardware Description _____

   Purchased From _____ Date _____

   Cost/Unit $_____ No. of Units _____ Total $_____

Notes: _____

FURNITURE/FIXTURES

Item	Purchased From	Date	Cost	Warranty

EXTRA NOTES

_____

_____

_____

_____

HALLWAY/STAIRWAY 2

FLOOR COVERING

Floor Measurements

Widest part of room from middle of doorway _____

Longest part of room from middle of doorway _____

Notes: _____

_____

Type & Material (nylon carpet, ceramic tile, etc.) _____

Purchased From _____ Date _____

Brand & Pattern _____

Color & No. _____ Warranty Period _____

Type of Backing _____ Pad Type _____

Cost/Unit $_____ No. of Units _____ Total $_____

Installed By _____ Attached With _____

Date _____ Cost $_____

Cleaned/Refinished By _____

Date 1 _____ Cost $_____

Date 2 _____ Cost $_____

Date 3 _____ Cost $_____

Notes: _____

_____

CEILING COVERING

Type of Covering (paint, spray texture, etc.) _____

Purchased From _____ Date _____

Brand & Pattern _____

Color & No. _____ Warranty Period _____

Applied with (texture roller, sprayer, etc.) _____

Cost/Unit $_____ No. of Units _____ Total $_____

Installed By _____

Date _____ Cost $_____

Notes: _____

_____

WINDOW COVERING

Window 1 Measurements

Height _____ Width _____ Top of Window to Floor _____ Trim Width ____

Type of Covering (draperies, blinds, etc.) _____

Purchased From _____ Cost $_____ Date _____

    Measurements of Window Covering _____

    Material & Cleaning Instructions _____

Cleaned By _____ Cost $_____ Date _____

Cleaned By _____ Cost $_____ Date _____

Notes: _____

WALL COVERING

Wall Measurements

    North _____ South _____ East _____ West _____

    Use "2nd Type of Covering" for woodwork or paneling. It has a "Refinished By" section.

1ˢᵗ Type of Covering (paint, paper, etc.) _____

Purchased From _____ Date _____

    Brand & Pattern _____

    Color & No. _____ Warranty Period _____

    Cost/Unit $_____ No. of Units _____ Total $_____

Installed By _____

    Date _____ Cost $_____

Notes: _____

2ⁿᵈ Type of Covering (paint, paper, etc.) _____

Purchased From _____ Date _____

    Brand & Pattern _____

    Color & No. _____ Warranty Period _____

    Cost/Unit $_____ No. of Units _____ Total $_____

Installed By _____

    Date _____ Cost $_____

Refinished By _____

    Date _____ Cost $_____

Notes: _____

SAMPLES: PAINT, WALLPAPER, ETC.

attach swatch or paint daub here

DOORS/TRIM

Purchased From _____ Date _____

   Brand & Style _____ Material (oak, steel, etc.)_____

   Stain/Paint Color & No. _____

    Finished With (polyurethane over stain, etc.) _____

Installed By _____ Total Cost $_____

Refinished By _____

   Refinished With _____

   Date _____ Cost $_____

Hardware Description _____

   Purchased From _____ Date _____

   Cost/Unit $_____ No. of Units _____ Total $_____

Notes: _____

FURNITURE/FIXTURES

Item	Purchased From	Date	Cost	Warranty

EXTRA NOTES

_____

_____

_____

_____

HALLWAY/STAIRWAY 3

FLOOR COVERING

Floor Measurements

Widest part of room from middle of doorway _____

Longest part of room from middle of doorway _____

Notes: _____

_____

Type & Material (nylon carpet, ceramic tile, etc.) _____

Purchased From _____ Date _____

Brand & Pattern _____

Color & No. _____ Warranty Period _____

Type of Backing _____ Pad Type _____

Cost/Unit $_____ No. of Units _____ Total $_____

Installed By _____ Attached With _____

Date _____ Cost $_____

Cleaned/Refinished By _____

Date 1 _____ Cost $_____

Date 2 _____ Cost $_____

Date 3 _____ Cost $_____

Notes: _____

_____

CEILING COVERING

Type of Covering (paint, spray texture, etc.) _____

Purchased From _____ Date _____

Brand & Pattern _____

Color & No. _____ Warranty Period _____

Applied with (texture roller, sprayer, etc.) _____

Cost/Unit $_____ No. of Units _____ Total $_____

Installed By _____

Date _____ Cost $_____

Notes: _____

_____

WINDOW COVERING

Window 1 Measurements

Height _____ Width _____ Top of Window to Floor _____ Trim Width _____

Type of Covering (draperies, blinds, etc.) _____

Purchased From _____ Cost $_____ Date _____

    Measurements of Window Covering _____

    Material & Cleaning Instructions _____

Cleaned By _____ Cost $_____ Date _____

Cleaned By _____ Cost $_____ Date _____

Notes: _____

WALL COVERING

Wall Measurements

    North _____ South _____ East _____ West _____

    Use "2nd Type of Covering" for woodwork or paneling. It has a "Refinished By" section.

1st Type of Covering (paint, paper, etc.) _____

Purchased From _____ Date _____

    Brand & Pattern _____

    Color & No. _____ Warranty Period _____

    Cost/Unit $_____ No. of Units _____ Total $_____

Installed By _____

    Date _____ Cost $_____

Notes: _____

2nd Type of Covering (paint, paper, etc.) _____

Purchased From _____ Date _____

    Brand & Pattern _____

    Color & No. _____ Warranty Period _____

    Cost/Unit $_____ No. of Units _____ Total $_____

Installed By _____

    Date _____ Cost $_____

Refinished By _____

    Date _____ Cost $_____

Notes: _____

SAMPLES: PAINT, WALLPAPER, ETC.

attach swatch or paint daub here

DOORS/TRIM

Purchased From _____ Date _____

Brand & Style _____ Material (oak, steel, etc.)_____

Stain/Paint Color & No. _____

Finished With (polyurethane over stain, etc.) _____

Installed By _____ Total Cost $_____

Refinished By _____

Refinished With _____

Date _____ Cost $ _____

Hardware Description _____

Purchased From _____ Date _____

Cost/Unit $_____ No. of Units _____ Total $_____

Notes: _____

FURNITURE/FIXTURES

Item	Purchased From	Date	Cost	Warranty

EXTRA NOTES

_____

_____

_____

_____

KITCHEN
FLOOR COVERING

Floor Measurements

    Widest part of room from middle of doorway _____

    Longest part of room from middle of doorway _____

    Notes: _____

_____

Type & Material (nylon carpet, ceramic tile, etc.) _____

Purchased From _____ Date _____

    Brand & Pattern _____

    Color & No. _____ Warranty Period _____

    Type of Backing _____ Pad Type _____

    Cost/Unit $_____ No. of Units _____ Total $_____

Installed By _____ Attached With _____

    Date _____ Cost $_____

Cleaned/Refinished By _____

    Date 1 _____ Cost $_____

    Date 2 _____ Cost $_____

    Date 3 _____ Cost $_____

Notes: _____

_____

CEILING COVERING

Type of Covering (paint, spray texture, etc.) _____

Purchased From _____ Date _____

    Brand & Pattern _____

    Color & No. _____ Warranty Period _____

    Applied with (texture roller, sprayer, etc.) _____

    Cost/Unit $_____ No. of Units _____ Total $_____

Installed By _____

    Date _____ Cost $_____

Notes: _____

_____

WINDOW COVERING

Window 1 Measurements

Height _____ Width _____ Top of Window to Floor _____ Trim Width _____

Type of Covering (draperies, blinds, etc.) _____

Purchased From _____ Cost $_____ Date _____

   Measurements of Window Covering _____

   Material & Cleaning Instructions _____

Cleaned By _____ Cost $_____ Date _____

Cleaned By _____ Cost $_____ Date _____

Notes: _____

_____

_____

Window 2 Measurements

Height _____ Width _____ Top of Window to Floor _____ Trim Width _____

Type of Covering (draperies, blinds, etc.) _____

Purchased From _____ Cost $_____ Date _____

   Measurements of Window Covering _____

   Material & Cleaning Instructions _____

Cleaned By _____ Cost $_____ Date _____

Notes: _____

_____

Window 3 Measurements

Height _____ Width _____ Top of Window to Floor _____ Trim Width _____

Type of Covering (draperies, blinds, etc.) _____

Purchased From _____ Cost $_____ Date _____

   Measurements of Window Covering _____

   Material & Cleaning Instructions _____

Cleaned By _____ Cost $_____ Date _____

Notes: _____

_____

WALL COVERING

Wall Measurements

North _____ South _____ East _____ West _____

Use "2nd Type of Covering" for woodwork or paneling. It has a "Refinished By" section.

1ˢᵗ Type of Covering (paint, paper, etc.) _____

Purchased From _____ Date _____

Brand & Pattern _____

Color & No. _____ Warranty Period _____

Cost/Unit $_____ No. of Units _____ Total $_____

Installed By _____

Date _____ Cost $_____

Notes: _____

_____

2ⁿᵈ Type of Covering (paint, paper, etc.) _____

Purchased From _____ Date _____

Brand & Pattern _____

Color & No. _____ Warranty Period _____

Cost/Unit $_____ No. of Units _____ Total $_____

Installed By _____

Date _____ Cost $_____

Refinished By _____

Date _____ Cost $_____

Notes: _____

_____

SAMPLES: PAINT, WALLPAPER, ETC.

attach swatch or paint daub here

CABINETS

Purchased From _____ Date _____

  Brand & Style _____ Material (oak, pine, etc.)_____

  Stain/Paint Color & No. _____

    Finished With (polyurethane over stain, etc.) _____

  Countertop Material _____

    Brand & Pattern _____ Color & No._____

Installed By _____ Total Cost $_____

Refinished By _____

  Refinished With _____

  Date _____ Cost $_____

Hardware Description _____

_____

  Purchased From _____ Date _____

  Cost/Unit $_____ No. of Units _____ Total $_____

Notes: _____

DOORS/TRIM

Purchased From _____ Date _____

  Brand & Style _____ Material (oak, steel, etc.)_____

  Stain/Paint Color & No. _____

    Finished With (polyurethane over stain, etc.) _____

Installed By _____ Total Cost $_____

Refinished By _____

  Refinished With _____

  Date _____ Cost $_____

Hardware Description _____

_____

  Purchased From _____ Date _____

  Cost/Unit $_____ No. of Units _____ Total $_____

Notes: _____

MAJOR APPLIANCES

Type (range, dishwasher, etc.) _____ Manufacturer _____

Model/Lot No. _____ Serial No. _____

Purchased From _____ Cost _____ Date _____

Authorized Service Center _____ Warranty Period _____

Maintenance/Service _____

Notes: _____

Type (range, dishwasher, etc.) _____ Manufacturer _____

Model/Lot No. _____ Serial No. _____

Purchased From _____ Cost _____ Date _____

Authorized Service Center _____ Warranty Period _____

Maintenance/Service _____

Notes: _____

Type (range, dishwasher, etc.) _____ Manufacturer _____

Model/Lot No. _____ Serial No. _____

Purchased From _____ Cost _____ Date _____

Authorized Service Center _____ Warranty Period _____

Maintenance/Service _____

Notes: _____

Type (range, dishwasher, etc.) _____ Manufacturer _____

Model/Lot No. _____ Serial No. _____

Purchased From _____ Cost _____ Date _____

Authorized Service Center _____ Warranty Period _____

Maintenance/Service _____

Notes: _____

Type (range, dishwasher, etc.) _____ Manufacturer _____

Model/Lot No. _____ Serial No. _____

Purchased From _____ Cost _____ Date _____

Authorized Service Center _____ Warranty Period _____

Maintenance/Service _____

Notes: _____

FURNITURE/FIXTURES/SMALL APPLIANCES

Item	Purchased From	Date	Cost	Warranty

EXTRA NOTES

(Use tick marks at top & bottom to make graph paper)

LAUNDRY ROOM

FLOOR COVERING

Floor Measurements

Widest part of room from middle of doorway _____

Longest part of room from middle of doorway _____

Notes: _____

_____

Type & Material (nylon carpet, ceramic tile, etc.) _____

Purchased From _____ Date _____

Brand & Pattern _____

Color & No. _____ Warranty Period _____

Type of Backing _____ Pad Type _____

Cost/Unit $_____ No. of Units _____ Total $_____

Installed By _____ Attached With _____

Date _____ Cost $_____

Cleaned/Refinished By _____

Date 1 _____ Cost $_____

Date 2 _____ Cost $_____

Date 3 _____ Cost $_____

Notes: _____

_____

CEILING COVERING

Type of Covering (paint, spray texture, etc.) _____

Purchased From _____ Date _____

Brand & Pattern _____

Color & No. _____ Warranty Period _____

Applied with (texture roller, sprayer, etc.) _____

Cost/Unit $_____ No. of Units _____ Total $_____

Installed By _____

Date _____ Cost $_____

Notes: _____

_____

LAUNDRY ROOM (continued)

WINDOW COVERING

Window 1 Measurements

Height _____ Width _____ Top of Window to Floor _____ Trim Width _____

Type of Covering (draperies, blinds, etc.) _____

Purchased From _____ Cost $_____ Date _____

    Measurements of Window Covering _____

    Material & Cleaning Instructions _____

Cleaned By _____ Cost $_____ Date _____

Cleaned By _____ Cost $_____ Date _____

Notes: _____

WALL COVERING

Wall Measurements

    North _____ South _____ East _____ West _____

    Use "2nd Type of Covering" for woodwork or paneling. It has a "Refinished By" section.

1st Type of Covering (paint, paper, etc.) _____

Purchased From _____ Date _____

    Brand & Pattern _____

    Color & No. _____ Warranty Period _____

    Cost/Unit $_____ No. of Units _____ Total $_____

Installed By _____

    Date _____ Cost $_____

Notes: _____

2nd Type of Covering (paint, paper, etc.) _____

Purchased From _____ Date _____

    Brand & Pattern _____

    Color & No. _____ Warranty Period _____

    Cost/Unit $_____ No. of Units _____ Total $_____

Installed By _____

    Date _____ Cost $_____

Refinished By _____

    Date _____ Cost $_____

Notes: _____

SAMPLES: PAINT, WALLPAPER, ETC.

attach swatch or paint daub here

MAJOR APPLIANCES

Type (washer, dryer, etc.) _____ Manufacturer _____

Model/Lot No. _____ Serial No. _____

Purchased From _____ Cost _____ Date _____

Authorized Service Center _____ Warranty Period _____

Maintenance/Service _____

Notes: _____

Type (washer, dryer, etc.) _____ Manufacturer _____

Model/Lot No. _____ Serial No. _____

Purchased From _____ Cost _____ Date _____

Authorized Service Center _____ Warranty Period _____

Maintenance/Service _____

Notes: _____

Type (washer, dryer, etc.) _____ Manufacturer _____

Model/Lot No. _____ Serial No. _____

Purchased From _____ Cost _____ Date _____

Authorized Service Center _____ Warranty Period _____

Maintenance/Service _____

Notes: _____

Type (washer, dryer, etc.) _____ Manufacturer _____

Model/Lot No. _____ Serial No. _____

Purchased From _____ Cost _____ Date _____

Authorized Service Center _____ Warranty Period _____

Maintenance/Service _____

Notes: _____

DOORS/TRIM

Purchased From _____ Date _____

    Brand & Style _____ Material (oak, steel, etc.)_____

    Stain/Paint Color & No. _____

      Finished With (polyurethane over stain, etc.) _____

Installed By _____ Total Cost $_____

Refinished By _____

    Refinished With _____

    Date _____ Cost $_____

Hardware Description _____

    Purchased From _____ Date _____

    Cost/Unit $_____ No. of Units _____ Total $_____

Notes: _____

FURNITURE/FIXTURES

Item	Purchased From	Date	Cost	Warranty

EXTRA NOTES

_____

_____

_____

_____

_____

_____

_____

_____

_____

LIVING ROOM

FLOOR COVERING

Floor Measurements

Widest part of room from middle of doorway _____

Longest part of room from middle of doorway _____

Notes: _____

_____

Type & Material (nylon carpet, ceramic tile, etc.) _____

Purchased From _____ Date _____

Brand & Pattern _____

Color & No. _____ Warranty Period _____

Type of Backing _____ Pad Type _____

Cost/Unit $_____ No. of Units _____ Total $_____

Installed By _____ Attached With _____

Date _____ Cost $_____

Cleaned/Refinished By _____

Date 1 _____ Cost $_____

Date 2 _____ Cost $_____

Date 3 _____ Cost $_____

Notes: _____

_____

CEILING COVERING

Type of Covering (paint, spray texture, etc.) _____

Purchased From _____ Date _____

Brand & Pattern _____

Color & No. _____ Warranty Period _____

Applied with (texture roller, sprayer, etc.) _____

Cost/Unit $_____ No. of Units _____ Total $_____

Installed By _____

Date _____ Cost $_____

Notes: _____

_____

WINDOW COVERING

Window 1 Measurements

Height _____ Width _____ Top of Window to Floor _____ Trim Width _____

Type of Covering (draperies, blinds, etc.) _____

Purchased From _____ Cost $_____ Date _____

    Measurements of Window Covering _____

    Material & Cleaning Instructions _____

Cleaned By _____ Cost $_____ Date _____

Cleaned By _____ Cost $_____ Date _____

Notes: _____

_____

_____

Window 2 Measurements

Height _____ Width _____ Top of Window to Floor _____ Trim Width _____

Type of Covering (draperies, blinds, etc.) _____

Purchased From _____ Cost $_____ Date _____

    Measurements of Window Covering _____

    Material & Cleaning Instructions _____

Cleaned By _____ Cost $_____ Date _____

Notes: _____

_____

Window 3 Measurements

Height _____ Width _____ Top of Window to Floor _____ Trim Width _____

Type of Covering (draperies, blinds, etc.) _____

Purchased From _____ Cost $_____ Date _____

    Measurements of Window Covering _____

    Material & Cleaning Instructions _____

Cleaned By _____ Cost $_____ Date _____

Notes: _____

_____

WALL COVERING

Wall Measurements

North _____ South _____ East _____ West _____

Use "2nd Type of Covering" for woodwork or paneling. It has a "Refinished By" section.

1st Type of Covering (paint, paper, etc.) _____

Purchased From _____ Date _____

Brand & Pattern _____

Color & No. _____ Warranty Period _____

Cost/Unit $_____ No. of Units _____ Total $_____

Installed By _____

Date _____ Cost $_____

Notes: _____

_____

2nd Type of Covering (paint, paper, etc.) _____

Purchased From _____ Date _____

Brand & Pattern _____

Color & No. _____ Warranty Period _____

Cost/Unit $_____ No. of Units _____ Total $_____

Installed By _____

Date _____ Cost $_____

Refinished By _____

Date _____ Cost $_____

Notes: _____

_____

SAMPLES: PAINT, WALLPAPER, ETC.

attach swatch or paint daub here

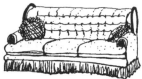

LIVING ROOM (continued)

DOORS/TRIM

Purchased From _____ Date _____

    Brand & Style _____ Material (oak, steel, etc.)_____

    Stain/Paint Color & No. _____

       Finished With (polyurethane over stain, etc.) _____

Installed By _____ Total Cost $_____

Refinished By _____

    Refinished With _____

    Date _____ Cost $_____

Hardware Description _____

_____

    Purchased From _____ Date _____

    Cost/Unit $_____ No. of Units _____ Total $_____

Notes: _____

_____

FURNITURE/FIXTURES

Item	Purchased From	Date	Cost	Warranty

EXTRA NOTES

(Use tick marks at top & bottom to make graph paper)

81

MISCELLANEOUS ROOM 1

FLOOR COVERING

Floor Measurements

Widest part of room from middle of doorway _____

Longest part of room from middle of doorway _____

Notes: _____

_____

Type & Material (nylon carpet, ceramic tile, etc.) _____

Purchased From _____ Date _____

Brand & Pattern _____

Color & No. _____ Warranty Period _____

Type of Backing _____ Pad Type _____

Cost/Unit $_____ No. of Units _____ Total $_____

Installed By _____ Attached With _____

Date _____ Cost $_____

Cleaned/Refinished By _____

Date 1 _____ Cost $_____

Date 2 _____ Cost $_____

Date 3 _____ Cost $_____

Notes: _____

_____

CEILING COVERING

Type of Covering (paint, spray texture, etc.) _____

Purchased From _____ Date _____

Brand & Pattern _____

Color & No. _____ Warranty Period _____

Applied with (texture roller, sprayer, etc.) _____

Cost/Unit $_____ No. of Units _____ Total $_____

Installed By _____

Date _____ Cost $_____

Notes: _____

_____

WINDOW COVERING

Window 1 Measurements

Height _____ Width _____ Top of Window to Floor _____ Trim Width _____

Type of Covering (draperies, blinds, etc.) _____

Purchased From _____ Cost $_____ Date _____

   Measurements of Window Covering _____

   Material & Cleaning Instructions _____

Cleaned By _____ Cost $_____ Date _____

Cleaned By _____ Cost $_____ Date _____

Notes: _____

_____

_____

Window 2 Measurements

Height _____ Width _____ Top of Window to Floor _____ Trim Width _____

Type of Covering (draperies, blinds, etc.) _____

Purchased From _____ Cost $_____ Date _____

   Measurements of Window Covering _____

   Material & Cleaning Instructions _____

Cleaned By _____ Cost $_____ Date _____

Notes: _____

_____

Window 3 Measurements

Height _____ Width _____ Top of Window to Floor _____ Trim Width _____

Type of Covering (draperies, blinds, etc.) _____

Purchased From _____ Cost $_____ Date _____

   Measurements of Window Covering _____

   Material & Cleaning Instructions _____

Cleaned By _____ Cost $_____ Date _____

Notes: _____

_____

WALL COVERING

Wall Measurements

North _____ South _____ East _____ West _____

Use "2nd Type of Covering" for woodwork or paneling. It has a "Refinished By" section.

1st Type of Covering (paint, paper, etc.) _____

Purchased From _____ Date _____

Brand & Pattern _____

Color & No. _____ Warranty Period _____

Cost/Unit $_____ No. of Units _____ Total $_____

Installed By _____

Date _____ Cost $_____

Notes: _____
_____

2nd Type of Covering (paint, paper, etc.) _____

Purchased From _____ Date _____

Brand & Pattern _____

Color & No. _____ Warranty Period _____

Cost/Unit $_____ No. of Units _____ Total $_____

Installed By _____

Date _____ Cost $_____

Refinished By _____

Date _____ Cost $_____

Notes: _____

SAMPLES: PAINT, WALLPAPER, ETC.

attach swatch or paint daub here

DOORS/TRIM

Purchased From _____ Date _____

   Brand & Style _____ Material (oak, steel, etc.)_____

   Stain/Paint Color & No. _____

    Finished With (polyurethane over stain, etc.) _____

Installed By _____ Total Cost $_____

Refinished By _____

   Refinished With _____

   Date _____ Cost $_____

Hardware Description _____

_____

   Purchased From _____ Date _____

   Cost/Unit $_____ No. of Units _____ Total $_____

Notes: _____

_____

FURNITURE/FIXTURES

Item	Purchased From	Date	Cost	Warranty

EXTRA NOTES
(Use tick marks at top & bottom to make graph paper)

MISCELLANEOUS ROOM 2

FLOOR COVERING

Floor Measurements

Widest part of room from middle of doorway _____

Longest part of room from middle of doorway _____

Notes: _____

_____

Type & Material (nylon carpet, ceramic tile, etc.) _____

Purchased From _____ Date _____

Brand & Pattern _____

Color & No. _____ Warranty Period _____

Type of Backing _____ Pad Type _____

Cost/Unit $_____ No. of Units _____ Total $_____

Installed By _____ Attached With _____

Date _____ Cost $_____

Cleaned/Refinished By _____

Date 1 _____ Cost $_____

Date 2 _____ Cost $_____

Date 3 _____ Cost $_____

Notes: _____

_____

CEILING COVERING

Type of Covering (paint, spray texture, etc.) _____

Purchased From _____ Date _____

Brand & Pattern _____

Color & No. _____ Warranty Period _____

Applied with (texture roller, sprayer, etc.) _____

Cost/Unit $_____ No. of Units _____ Total $_____

Installed By _____

Date _____ Cost $_____

Notes: _____

_____

WINDOW COVERING

Window 1 Measurements

Height _____ Width _____ Top of Window to Floor _____ Trim Width _____

Type of Covering (draperies, blinds, etc.) _____

Purchased From _____ Cost $_____ Date _____

    Measurements of Window Covering _____

    Material & Cleaning Instructions _____

Cleaned By _____ Cost $_____ Date _____

Cleaned By _____ Cost $_____ Date _____

Notes: _____

_____

_____

Window 2 Measurements

Height _____ Width _____ Top of Window to Floor _____ Trim Width _____

Type of Covering (draperies, blinds, etc.) _____

Purchased From _____ Cost $_____ Date _____

    Measurements of Window Covering _____

    Material & Cleaning Instructions _____

Cleaned By _____ Cost $_____ Date _____

Notes: _____

_____

Window 3 Measurements

Height _____ Width _____ Top of Window to Floor _____ Trim Width _____

Type of Covering (draperies, blinds, etc.) _____

Purchased From _____ Cost $_____ Date _____

    Measurements of Window Covering _____

    Material & Cleaning Instructions _____

Cleaned By _____ Cost $_____ Date _____

Notes: _____

_____

WALL COVERING

Wall Measurements

North _____ South _____ East _____ West _____

Use "2nd Type of Covering" for woodwork or paneling. It has a "Refinished By" section.

1st Type of Covering (paint, paper, etc.) _____

Purchased From _____ Date _____

    Brand & Pattern _____

    Color & No. _____ Warranty Period _____

    Cost/Unit $_____ No. of Units _____ Total $_____

Installed By _____

    Date _____ Cost $_____

Notes: _____

_____

2nd Type of Covering (paint, paper, etc.) _____

Purchased From _____ Date _____

    Brand & Pattern _____

    Color & No. _____ Warranty Period _____

    Cost/Unit $_____ No. of Units _____ Total $_____

Installed By _____

    Date _____ Cost $_____

Refinished By _____

    Date _____ Cost $_____

Notes: _____

_____

SAMPLES: PAINT, WALLPAPER, ETC.

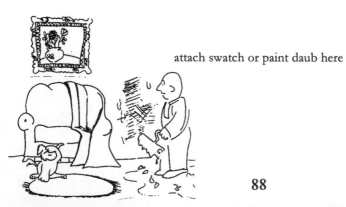

attach swatch or paint daub here

DOORS/TRIM

Purchased From _____ Date _____

    Brand & Style _____ Material (oak, steel, etc.)_____

    Stain/Paint Color & No. _____

       Finished With (polyurethane over stain, etc.) _____

Installed By _____ Total Cost $_____

Refinished By _____

    Refinished With _____

    Date _____ Cost $_____

Hardware Description _____

_____

    Purchased From _____ Date _____

    Cost/Unit $_____ No. of Units _____ Total $_____

Notes: _____

_____

FURNITURE/FIXTURES

Item	Purchased From	Date	Cost	Warranty

EXTRA NOTES

(Use tick marks at top & bottom to make graph paper)

MISCELLANEOUS ROOM 3

FLOOR COVERING

Floor Measurements

Widest part of room from middle of doorway _____

Longest part of room from middle of doorway _____

Notes: _____

_____

Type & Material (nylon carpet, ceramic tile, etc.) _____

Purchased From _____ Date _____

Brand & Pattern _____

Color & No. _____ Warranty Period _____

Type of Backing _____ Pad Type _____

Cost/Unit $_____ No. of Units _____ Total $_____

Installed By _____ Attached With _____

Date _____ Cost $_____

Cleaned/Refinished By _____

Date 1 _____ Cost $_____

Date 2 _____ Cost $_____

Date 3 _____ Cost $_____

Notes: _____

_____

CEILING COVERING

Type of Covering (paint, spray texture, etc.) _____

Purchased From _____ Date _____

Brand & Pattern _____

Color & No. _____ Warranty Period _____

Applied with (texture roller, sprayer, etc.) _____

Cost/Unit $_____ No. of Units _____ Total $_____

Installed By _____

Date _____ Cost $_____

Notes: _____

_____

WINDOW COVERING

Window 1 Measurements

Height _____ Width _____ Top of Window to Floor _____ Trim Width _____

Type of Covering (draperies, blinds, etc.) _____

Purchased From _____ Cost $_____ Date _____

   Measurements of Window Covering _____

   Material & Cleaning Instructions _____

Cleaned By _____ Cost $_____ Date _____

Cleaned By _____ Cost $_____ Date _____

Notes: _____

_____

_____

Window 2 Measurements

Height _____ Width _____ Top of Window to Floor _____ Trim Width _____

Type of Covering (draperies, blinds, etc.) _____

Purchased From _____ Cost $ Date

   Measurements of Window Covering _____

   Material & Cleaning Instructions _____

Cleaned By _____ Cost $_____ Date _____

Notes: _____

_____

Window 3 Measurements

Height _____ Width _____ Top of Window to Floor _____ Trim Width _____

Type of Covering (draperies, blinds, etc.) _____

Purchased From _____ Cost $_____ Date _____

   Measurements of Window Covering _____

   Material & Cleaning Instructions _____

Cleaned By _____ Cost $_____ Date _____

Notes: _____

_____

WALL COVERING

Wall Measurements

North _____ South _____ East _____ West _____

Use "2nd Type of Covering" for woodwork or paneling. It has a "Refinished By" section.

1st Type of Covering (paint, paper, etc.) _____

Purchased From _____ Date _____

Brand & Pattern _____

Color & No. _____ Warranty Period _____

Cost/Unit $_____ No. of Units _____ Total $_____

Installed By _____

Date _____ Cost $_____

Notes: _____

_____

2nd Type of Covering (paint, paper, etc.) _____

Purchased From _____ Date _____

Brand & Pattern _____

Color & No. _____ Warranty Period _____

Cost/Unit $_____ No. of Units _____ Total $_____

Installed By _____

Date _____ Cost $_____

Refinished By _____

Date _____ Cost $_____

Notes: _____

_____

SAMPLES: PAINT, WALLPAPER, ETC.

attach swatch or paint daub here

DOORS/TRIM

Purchased From _____ Date _____

    Brand & Style _____ Material (oak, steel, etc.)_____

    Stain/Paint Color & No. _____

       Finished With (polyurethane over stain, etc.) _____

Installed By _____ Total Cost $_____

Refinished By _____

    Refinished With _____

    Date _____ Cost $_____

Hardware Description _____

_____

    Purchased From _____ Date _____

    Cost/Unit $_____ No. of Units _____ Total $_____

Notes: _____

_____

FURNITURE/FIXTURES

Item	Purchased From	Date	Cost	Warranty

EXTRA NOTES

(Use tick marks at top & bottom to make graph paper)

STORAGE/CLOSETS

_____

_____

_____

_____

_____

_____

_____

_____

_____

_____

_____

_____

_____

_____

_____

_____

_____

_____

_____

_____

_____

_____

_____

_____

_____

_____

_____

_____

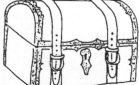

DECK

Type of Wood (redwood, green treated, etc.) _____

Purchased From _____ Date _____

Sealed/Finished With (brand, type, color, no.) _____

Misc. Materials _____ Cost $_____

Installed By _____ Total $_____

Refinished With _____ Date _____

    Contractor _____ Cost $_____

Refinished With _____ Date _____

    Contractor _____ Cost $_____

Refinished With _____ Date _____

    Contractor _____ Cost $_____

Notes: _____

_____

DRIVEWAY

Type of Driveway (asphalt, concrete, etc.) _____

Installed By _____ Cost $_____ Date _____

Sealed With (brand, type, & no.) _____

    Purchased From/Contractor _____ Date _____

    Cost/Unit $_____ No. of Units _____ Total $_____

Sealed With (brand, type, & no.) _____

    Purchased From/Contractor _____ Date _____

    Cost/Unit $_____ No. of Units _____ Total $_____

Sealed With (brand, type, & no.) _____

    Purchased From/Contractor _____ Date _____

    Cost/Unit $_____ No. of Units _____ Total $_____

Sealed With (brand, type, & no.) _____

    Purchased From/Contractor _____ Date _____

    Cost/Unit $_____ No. of Units _____ Total $_____

    Notes: _____

_____

FENCES

1st Fence Type of Material (redwood, wire, etc.) _____

Purchased From _____ Date _____

Finished With (brand, type, color, no.) _____

Installed By _____ Total $_____ Date _____

Refinished With _____ Date _____

    Contractor _____ Cost $_____

Refinished With _____ Date _____

    Contractor _____ Cost $_____

Notes: _____

_____

_____

_____

2nd Fence Type of Material (redwood, wire, etc.) _____

Purchased From _____ Date _____

Finished With (brand, type, color, no.) _____

Installed By _____ Total $_____ Date _____

Refinished With _____ Date _____

    Contractor _____ Cost $_____

Refinished With _____ Date _____

    Contractor _____ Cost $_____

Notes: _____

_____

_____

_____

GAZEBO

_____

_____

_____

_____

_____

_____

_____

PATIO

Type of Material (patio blocks, cement, etc.) _____

Installed By _____ Total $_____ Date _____

Sealed With (brand, type, & no.) _____

    Contractor _____ Cost $_____ Date _____

Sealed With (brand, type, & no.) _____

    Contractor _____ Cost $_____ Date _____

Notes: _____

_____

PORCH

(Use tick marks at top & bottom to make graph paper)

STORAGE SHEDS/OUTBUILDINGS

GARAGE
FLOOR

Type of Floor (asphalt, concrete, etc.) _____

Installed By _____ Cost $_____ Date _____

Sealed/Finished With (brand, type, & no.) _____

    Purchased From _____ Date _____

    Cost/Unit $_____ No. of Units _____ Total $_____

Maintenance _____

_____

Notes: _____

_____

GUTTERS & DOWNSPOUTS

Type of Material (steel, vinyl, etc.) _____ Warranty Period _____

Purchased From _____ Date _____

Cost/Unit $_____ No. of Units _____ Total $_____

Installed By _____ Cost $_____ Date _____

Notes: _____

_____

_____

ROOF

Type of Roofing (fiberglass shingles, cedar shakes, etc.) _____

Purchased From _____ Date _____ Warranty Period _____

    Brand, Color & No. _____

    Cost/Unit $_____ No. of Units _____ Total $_____

Misc. Materials _____ Cost $_____

Installed By _____ Cost $_____ Date _____

Total Materials Cost $ _____ Entire Job Cost $_____

Maintenance (preservative, repairs, etc.) _____

_____

Notes: _____

_____

_____

SIDING

<u>**1st Type of Siding**</u> (brick, stucco, etc.) _____

Supplier _____ Date _____ Warranty Period _____

    Brand, Color, & No. _____

    Cost/Unit $_____ No. of Units _____ Total $_____

Type of Finish (paint, stain, etc.) _____

    Cost/Unit $_____ No. of Units _____ Total $_____

    Purchased From _____ Date _____ Warranty Period _____

Installed By _____ Cost $_____ Date _____

Notes: _____

_____

_____

_____

_____

_____

_____

<u>**2nd Type of Siding**</u> (brick, stucco, etc.) _____

Supplier _____ Date _____ Warranty Period _____

    Brand, Color, & No. _____

    Cost/Unit $_____ No. of Units _____ Total $_____

Type of Finish (paint, stain, etc.) _____

    Cost/Unit $_____ No. of Units _____ Total $_____

    Purchased From _____ Date _____ Warranty Period _____

Installed By _____ Cost $_____ Date _____

Notes: _____

_____

_____

_____

_____

_____

_____

_____

TRIM

<u>1st Type of Trim</u> (wood, vinyl, etc.) _____

Supplier _____ Date _____ Warranty Period _____

   Brand, Color, & No. _____

   Cost/Unit $_____ No. of Units _____ Total $_____

Type of Finish (paint, stain, etc.) _____

   Cost/Unit $_____ No. of Units _____ Total $_____

   Purchased From _____ Date _____ Warranty Period _____

Installed By _____ Cost $_____ Date _____

Notes: _____

_____

_____

<u>2nd Type of Trim</u> (wood, vinyl, etc.) _____

Supplier _____ Date _____ Warranty Period _____

   Brand, Color, & No. _____

   Cost/Unit $_____ No. of Units _____ Total $_____

Type of Finish (paint, stain, etc.) _____

   Cost/Unit $_____ No. of Units _____ Total $_____

   Purchased From _____ Date _____ Warranty Period _____

Installed By _____ Cost $_____ Date _____

Notes: _____

WALLS & CEILING

<u>Type of Material</u> (gypsum board, etc.) _____

Purchased From _____ Date _____ Warranty Period _____

   Cost/Unit $_____ No. of Units _____ Total $_____

   Sealed/Finished With (brand, color, & no.) _____

Notes: _____

_____

_____

HOUSE EXTERIOR
GUTTERS & DOWNSPOUTS

Type of Material (steel, vinyl, etc.) _____ Warranty Period _____

Purchased From _____ Date _____

Cost/Unit $_____ No. of Units _____ Total $_____

Installed By _____ Cost $_____ Date _____

Notes: _____

_____

_____

_____

_____

ROOF

Type of Roofing (fiberglass shingles, cedar shakes, etc.) _____

Purchased From _____ Date _____ Warranty Period _____

Brand, Color & No. _____

Cost/Unit $_____ No. of Units _____ Total $_____

Misc. Materials _____ Cost $_____

Installed By _____ Cost $_____ Date _____

Total Materials Cost $ _____ Entire Job Cost $_____

Maintenance (preservative, repairs, etc.) _____

_____

_____

Notes: _____

_____

_____

_____

STORM DOORS

_____

_____

_____

_____

_____

SIDING

1st Type of Siding (brick, stucco, etc.) _____

Supplier _____ Date _____ Warranty Period _____

Brand, Color, & No. _____

Cost/Unit $_____ No. of Units _____ Total $_____

Type of Finish (paint, stain, etc.) _____

Cost/Unit $_____ No. of Units _____ Total $_____

Purchased From _____ Date _____ Warranty Period _____

Installed By _____ Cost $_____ Date _____

Notes: _____

_____

_____

2nd Type of Siding (brick, stucco, etc.) _____

Supplier _____ Date _____ Warranty Period _____

Brand, Color, & No. _____

Cost/Unit $_____ No. of Units _____ Total $_____

Type of Finish (paint, stain, etc.) _____

Cost/Unit $_____ No. of Units _____ Total $_____

Purchased From _____ Date _____ Warranty Period _____

Installed By _____ Cost $_____ Date _____

Notes: _____

_____

_____

STORM WINDOWS

Type of Frame (wood, vinyl, etc.) _____

(Use "Trim" on next page for "Type of Finish")

Purchased From _____ Date _____ Warranty Period _____

Cost/Unit $_____ No. of Units _____ Total $_____

Installed By _____ Cost $_____ Date _____

Notes: _____

_____

_____

TRIM

__1st Type of Trim__ (wood, vinyl, etc.) _____

Supplier _____ Date _____ Warranty Period _____

  Brand, Color, & No. _____

  Cost/Unit $_____ No. of Units _____ Total $_____

Type of Finish (paint, stain, etc.) _____

  Cost/Unit $_____ No. of Units _____ Total $_____

  Purchased From _____ Date _____ Warranty Period _____

Installed By _____ Cost $_____ Date _____

Notes: _____
_____
_____
_____

__2nd Type of Trim__ (wood, vinyl, etc.) _____

Supplier _____ Date _____ Warranty Period _____

  Brand, Color, & No. _____

  Cost/Unit $_____ No. of Units _____ Total $_____

Type of Finish (paint, stain, etc.) _____

  Cost/Unit $_____ No. of Units _____ Total $_____

  Purchased From _____ Date _____ Warranty Period _____

Installed By _____ Cost $_____ Date _____

Notes: _____
_____

EXTRA NOTES

_____
_____
_____
_____
_____
_____

COOLING & HEATING
AIR CONDITIONER

Type of Unit (electric, natural gas, etc.) _____

Manufacturer & Model _____ Efficiency _____

Purchased From/Contractor _____ Date _____

    Cost $_____ Warranty Period _____

    Filter Type _____ Size _____

Cleaned/Serviced By _____

    Date No. 1 _____ Cost $_____

    Date No. 2 _____ Cost $_____

    Date No. 3 _____ Cost $_____

    Date No. 4 _____ Cost $_____

Notes: _____

_____

FIREPLACE

Insert Mfr. & Model _____

Purchased From _____ Date _____

    Cost $_____ Warranty Period _____

Installed By _____ Cost $_____ Date _____

Chimney Cleaned By _____

    Date No. 1 _____ Cost $_____

    Date No. 2 _____ Cost $_____

Notes: _____

_____

HEAT EXCHANGER

Manufacturer & Model _____ Efficiency _____

Purchased From _____ Date _____

    Cost $_____ Warranty Period _____

Installed By _____ Cost $_____ Date _____

Cleaned/Serviced By _____ Cost $_____ Date _____

Notes: _____

_____

HEAT PUMP

Type of Unit (electric, fuel oil, etc.) _____

Manufacturer & Model _____ Efficiency _____

Purchased From/Contractor _____ Date _____

    Cost $_____ Warranty Period _____

    Filter Type _____ Size _____

Cleaned/Serviced By _____

    Date No. 1 _____ Cost $_____

    Date No. 2 _____ Cost $_____

Notes: _____

HEATING PLANT (Furnace)

Type of Unit (electric, fuel oil, etc.) _____

Manufacturer & Model _____ Efficiency _____

Purchased From/Contractor _____ Date _____

    Cost $_____ Warranty Period _____

    Filter Type _____ Size _____

    Humidifier _____

Cleaned/Serviced By _____

    Date No. 1 _____ Cost $_____

    Date No. 2 _____ Cost $_____

    Date No. 3 _____ Cost $_____

    Date No. 4 _____ Cost $_____

Notes: _____

WOOD STOVE

Manufacturer & Model _____ Efficiency _____

Purchased From/Contractor _____ Date _____

    Cost $_____ Warranty Period _____

Chimney Cleaned By _____

    Date No. 1 _____ Cost $_____

    Date No. 2 _____ Cost $_____

Notes: _____

INSULATION
ATTIC

Type of Insulation (fiberglass rolls, etc.) _____

    Thickness _____ R-Value Added _____ Cost $_____

    Previous R-Value _____ Aggregate R-Value _____

    Type of Vapor Barrier (6 mill poly, etc.) _____

Installed By _____ Date _____

Total Material Cost $_____ Labor $_____ Total $_____

Notes: _____

_____

_____

Type of Venting   Note: You should have one square foot of free-flowing cross-ventilation for every 150 square feet. of attic floor space. Soffit vents with screen covers can reduce air flow by up to 75%.

Under Eave (Soffit) Sq. In./cm _____ Louvered Attic Vents Sq. In./cm _____

Low Pitch Slant Roof Vents Sq. In./cm _____ Turbines Sq. In./cm _____

Other _____

Notes: _____

_____

_____

WALLS

1ˢᵗ Type of Insulation (fiberglass rolls, etc.) _____

    Thickness _____ R-Value Added _____ Cost $_____

2nd Type of Insulation (fiberglass rolls, etc.) _____

    Thickness _____ R-Value Added _____ Cost $_____

Aggregate R-Value _____ Warranty Period _____

Type of Vapor Barrier (6 mill poly, etc.) _____

Installed By _____ Date _____

Total Material Cost $_____ Labor $_____ Total $_____

Notes: _____

_____

_____

_____

OTHER INSULATION
(rim joist, exterior foundation, etc.)

DOOR CHIMES

GARAGE DOOR OPENERS

INTERCOM SYSTEM

SECURITY SYSTEM

SMOKE/FIRE DETECTORS

TELEPHONES/ANSWERING MACHINE/FAX

THERMOSTATS

RADON TESTING & INFORMATION

SEWER/CESSPOOL/SEPTIC SYSTEM

SUMP PUMP

SWIMMING POOL

WATER HEATERS

WATER SOFTENER

WELL

WHIRLPOOL/HOT TUB/SAUNA

WHOLE HOUSE VACUUM

GARDENING/LANDSCAPING
GARDEN DIARY/PHENOLOGY

(Record special events or occurrences around your home, such as the all-time earliest day you've ever sighted a robin, or picked that first tomato of the season. If you live in a colder climate, you might want to record the largest snowfall. Use pencil to allow for easy updates)

1st/Earliest _____

1st/Earliest _____

Last _____

Last _____

Most rain _____

Heat wave/highest temp. _____

Cold wave/coldest temp. _____

Last snow/most snow _____

Record vegetable size or harvest _____

_____

Bird sightings _____

_____

_____

_____

Wildlife sightings _____

_____

_____

Other _____

_____

_____

_____

_____

_____

_____

_____

_____

_____

_____

GARDEN/YARD DIAGRAMS

(Use tick marks on lines to make graph paper to create one large diagram, or a few small diagrams for individual flowerbeds. Use any leftover space for notes.)

TREES/SHRUBS/PERENNIALS

Plant Type	Size	Qty.	Cost	Date	Supplier

Special Care/Notes: _____

Special Care/Notes: _____

Special Care/Notes: _____

Special Care/Notes: _____

Special Care/Notes: _____

Special Care/Notes: _____

Plant Type	Size	Qty.	Cost	Date	Supplier

Special Care/Notes: _____

Special Care/Notes: _____

Special Care/Notes: _____

Special Care/Notes: _____

Special Care/Notes: _____

Special Care/Notes: _____

WATERFALL/WATER GARDEN/FOUNTAIN

<u>Type</u> (waterfall, self-contained fountain, etc.) _____

Material	Qty.	Cost	Date	Warranty	Supplier

Pump _____ Size _____ Cost _____ Date _____ Warranty _____

Electrical/Lights _____

Purchased from _____ Cost _____ Date _____ Warranty _____

Installed by _____ Cost _____ Date _____

Cleaning _____

Chemical Treatment _____

Maintenance _____

Plant Type	Qty.	Cost	Date	Supplier

Fish Type	Size	Qty.	Cost	Date	Supplier

EQUIPMENT

(Tractors, mowers, snow blowers, etc.)

Type _____ Mfr. _____ Model _____ Serial No. _____

Purchased From _____ Cost _____ Date _____ Warranty _____

Maintenance/Service _____

_____

_____

_____

Notes: _____

_____

Type _____ Mfr. _____ Model _____ Serial No. _____

Purchased From _____ Cost _____ Date _____ Warranty _____

Maintenance/Service _____

_____

_____

_____

Notes: _____

_____

Type _____ Mfr. _____ Model _____ Serial No. _____

Purchased From _____ Cost _____ Date _____ Warranty _____

Maintenance/Service _____

_____

_____

_____

Notes: _____

_____

Type _____ Mfr. _____ Model _____ Serial No. _____

Purchased From _____ Cost _____ Date _____ Warranty _____

Maintenance/Service _____

_____

_____

Notes: _____

PORTABLE (luggable) ITEMS

ARBOR/TRELLIS/LATTICE

_____

_____

BARBEQUE/GRILL

_____

_____

BIRD FEEDERS & BATHS/WILDLIFE FEEDERS

_____

_____

_____

_____

COMPOST BIN

_____

LAWN FURNITURE/PICNIC TABLE

_____

_____

_____

LAWN SWING/GLIDER

_____

_____

LIGHTING-OUTDOOR

_____

_____

_____

_____

ORNAMENTS/STATUARY/FLOWER BOXES

_____
_____
_____
_____
_____

RETAINING WALLS

(The tick marks at top & bottom can be used to make graph paper to diagram walls)

_____
_____
_____
_____
_____
_____
_____
_____

SWING & PLAY SETS/SAND BOX

_____
_____

WHEELBARROWS/CARTS/PLANTING TABLES

_____
_____

YARD TOOLS/EQUIPMENT

_____
_____
_____
_____

LAWN/GARDEN IRRIGATION & SERVICE

GARDEN IRRIGATION

(The tick marks at top & bottom can be used to make graph paper to diagram system)

LAWN MAINTENANCE/SERVICE

SPRINKLER SYSTEM

(The tick marks at top & bottom can be used to make graph paper to diagram system)

WATERING SCHEDULE

GARDEN/YARD MISCELLANEOUS
BURIED CABLE/PIPELINE LOCATIONS

EDGING

MULCH

PESTS (insects, animals, not neighbors)

SOIL SAMPLES

WEED BARRIER

TAX IMPLICATIONS OF SELLING YOUR HOME

Notice: *This is a general overview of the tax concepts to consider when buying and selling your principal residence. It is not intended to be a complete discussion of all the tax implications of selling your home, which vary regionally. If you have any questions, seek the advice of a qualified tax professional.*

You can generally exclude from income up to $250,000 of gain ($500,000 for joint filers) from the sale of the home that you own and have used as your principal residence for at least 2 of the 5 years before the sale. The full exclusion doesn't apply if, within the 2-year period ending on the sale date, you had another home sale to which the exclusion applied. However, a partial exclusion may apply if you must sell your home due to a change of place of employment, health, or to other unforeseen circumstances.

In the event that you do not qualify for the capital gain exclusion, you can still minimize your income taxes by keeping the proper information to calculate the tax basis of your home. The tax basis of your home is the amount paid for your home plus miscellaneous costs associated with the purchase of a home (appraisal fees, title cost, etc.), plus subsequent improvements.

Subsequent improvements include items such as finishing the basement, adding additional rooms, replacing the furnace, installing an air conditioning system, replacing the roof, landscaping, fencing, swimming pools, etc. Repairs, on the other hand, are not included in the tax basis of your home. Repairs include items such as painting, re-coating the driveway, replacing broken windows, repairing or replacing electrical fixtures, etc. However, if repairs were done as part of a larger renovation of your home, they would be included in the renovation costs and could then be added to the tax basis.

In calculating the tax basis of your home, include the original cost of your home plus any subsequent improvements. When you sell your home, the Internal Revenue Service requires that you have sufficient documentation to substantiate the tax basis. Sufficient documentation includes the closing papers on the purchase of your home and invoices and receipts for any improvements you made. You will need the invoices from the contractors showing the date the improvements were made, what was done, and how much it cost. If you do the work yourself, you will need to keep receipts for materials. Also, if you do the work yourself, you cannot add your own labor to the tax basis.

The following pages are included to record the improvements made to your home. When an improvement is made, record the date, description, and amount. Remember that you need to keep the supporting documentation (invoices and receipts) to substantiate these items.

Special thanks for this tax information goes to the certified public accounting firm of Mathwig & Whipps, P.A., located in Apple Valley, Minnesota.

TAX WORKSHEET

Amount

Original Cost of Home Per Purchase Agreement _____

Add Closing Costs:

    Legal Fees _____

    Appraisal Fee _____

    Commission Fee to Broker _____

    Escrow Fee _____

    Title Cost _____

    State Deed Taxes and Filing Fees _____

    Loan Placement Fees (e.g. Points) _____

    Other _____

Add Remodeling and Renovations Made:

Date	Description	Amount

Add Improvements Made:

Date	Description	Amount

HOW TO FILE IMPORTANT PAPERS

Every home owner needs a good home filing system for keeping important documents and receipts for tax, insurance, warranty, or budget purposes. A good system will also save you a great deal of money, time, and aggravation. Take time in the beginning to set up the system that is right for you. The right system will be easy to use and allow for easy retrieval of documents. A system that is too primitive is no better than throwing all receipts into a shoebox. Conversely, a filing system that is too complex will be a chore to use.

After considerable research and experimentation, I developed a filing system that is easy to use, easy on my time, flexible, and inexpensive to start. All it consists of is:

1. Two large expanding folders with individual pockets and preprinted alphabetic tabs: (1) one set is for filing papers dealing with the purchase of your home and any work done on your home and (2) the other set is to file receipts for things you buy for your home and family. Two file systems eliminate what could be a huge sorting problem when tax information must be separated from ordinary purchases.

2. A household inventory for insurance purposes.

The supplies for this system are inexpensive, especially when compared to the money, time, and patience you may lose without them. They are available in many book, office supply, and variety stores.

Label one file set "Home Owner's Journal." This set is for filing papers dealing with the *purchase of your home* and any *work done on your home*. Keep only photocopies of important receipts in this file (put the originals in your safe-deposit box). Include receipts for budgeting, planning, and tax purposes (see the Tax Implications of Selling Your Home chapter). This file should also contain copies of purchase agreements and other closing documents from the purchase your home, receipts for repairs, additions, installation, purchases, care or cleaning instructions, contractor business cards, etc.

File each item under the appropriate letter in the alphabet. For example, living room carpet receipts, warranties, care instructions, the installer's business card, etc. should be stapled together, labeled "living room carpet," and filed under "C" for carpet. Don't forget to make appropriate notes on the documents such as "date purchased," if they are not already marked.

If you are not sure where to file something, put it in the most obvious place and put a "See _____" cross-reference note where it could also be filed.

126

Periodically purge the file of information you no longer need, such as expired warranties and receipts for old paint you wallpapered over.

The second file set should be labeled "Purchases." This set is for all the receipts, care and cleaning instructions, warranty cards, serial numbers, and instruction booklets for things you buy for your home and family such as appliances, electronics, furniture, wrist watches, etc. File each of these items under the appropriate letter of the alphabet. Follow the same filing instructions as in the previous paragraphs.

It is a good idea to maintain a written inventory of the contents of your home for insurance purposes in case of fire or burglary. A written inventory is perhaps easiest done with a good home inventory journal that can be found in book, office supply, and variety stores. Look for one that allows you some flexibility. Many books are so specific that much of the book is wasted with items that don't apply to you. Some can also leave you short of room for the things you do have. If you are very thorough, a tablet will also work.

Photographs or a video tape are good complements too, but not substitutes for the written inventory. They help show the condition of the item, which is important if you have an "actual cash value" insurance policy (which is often based on the depreciated value) instead of the "replacement value." Ask your insurance agent which type you have. The difference in your premium may not be that much and replacement cost is often well worth the difference.

Another alternative to paper is a tape recorder. As with video tape, however, updates are difficult to make unless added to the end of the tape.

Whichever method you choose, make sure it fits into your safe deposit box. That is where you should keep it once it is complete. Update it whenever necessary, but return it when finished. Keep a copy at home for reference.

EXTRA NOTES

(Use tick marks at top & bottom to make graph paper)

EXTRA NOTES

(Use tick marks at top & bottom to make graph paper)

EXTRA NOTES

(Use tick marks at top & bottom to make graph paper)

EXTRA NOTES

(Use tick marks at top & bottom to make graph paper)

EXTRA NOTES

(Use tick marks at top & bottom to make graph paper)

INDEX

OTHER BLUE SKY MARKETING INC. BOOKS

Reflections of a Small Town Santa: A True Story About Santa Claus
by Bob Litak

The wonderful, remarkable, and touching story of how, for twelve years, the author exchanged his lawyer's briefcase for a Santa sack and played Santa to the children of a small town. This book will soften even the hardest hearts! Hardcover, 98 pages, 5x7.

101 Questions About Santa Claus (As Answered by Santa Himself!)
Accurately recorded by Bob Litak

Santa answers those tough questions with ease, such as "How do Santa's reindeer fly?", "What if a home has no chimney?" and 99 other questions commonly asked of Santa. Hardcover, 128 pages, 5x7.

Master Dating®: How to Meet and Attract Quality Men!
by Felicia Rose Adler

Written in a refreshing style, *Master Dating*® is full of powerful, practical insights designed to help the over 40 million single women in America attain their ideal love life. This book dissects and dismantles every obstacle that stands between women and love. Follow the author's sound advice and you'll soon be living the love life you desire. Softcover, 192 pages, 5 ½ x 8 ½.

31 Days To *Increase* Your Stress
by Tricia Seymour, MA, LPC, LMFT

Yes, you read it right! This (tongue-in-cheek) book tells you how you can *increase* your stress to epic levels in as little as 31 days! (or take the more sensible approach and do the opposite to *lower* your stress level.) Softcover, 80 pages, 6x4.

31 Days to RUIN Your Relationship
by Tricia Seymour & Rusty Barrier

Yes, you read that right too! The authors of this clever, fun-to-read gift book again use the humorous, reverse psychology approach to help people improve their relationships (if they do the *opposite* of what the author's say). Softcover, 80 pages, 6x4.

Vacation Getaway: A Journal for Your Travel Memories

The easiest to use travel diary on the market! Convenient to carry (fits into a purse or jacket pocket) travel diary allows travelers to easily record & preserve the daily highlights of their trips. Includes 14 top-opening pockets to hold receipts, postcards, photographs, and other mementos for each day. Also includes 2 expense tracking pages. Softcover (spiral wire binding), 36 pages (including pockets), 5x9.

Money & Time-Saving Household Hints

Featured on ABC television's "Home Show." Packed with over 1,000 clever, useful, and sometimes startling solutions to everyday problems, this national best-seller in Canada is now available in the U.S.! *Household Hints* provides new solutions to everything from how to put the "bounce" back into old tennis balls to an astonishing way to make ferns grow faster! Softcover, 128 pages, 6x9.

It's So Cold™ In Wisconsin...
by Bonnie Stewart & Cathy McGlynn

'It's So Cold™ In Wisconsin... people pay extra for warm beer.'
This is one of the 90+ quips in this hilarious book. Most are absolutely true, although only a Wisonsinite would know for sure! They're great gifts for fair weather relatives and friends or just to pass time waiting for the tow truck to pull you out of the ditch. Softcover, 96 pages, 6x4

It's So Cold™ In Minnesota...
by Bonnie Stewart & Cathy McGlynn

'...your car finally starts blowing warm air just as you pull into the parking lot at work.' The huge Minnesota best seller! So, how *do* Minnesotans survive their winters? They poke fun at it by seeing how many humorous endings they can tag onto the expression "It's So Cold In Minnesota..." Great gift for fair weather friends. Softcover, 96 pgs, 6x4

The Weekly Menu Planner & Shopping List

In one easy step, busy cooks can plan a week's worth of meals and have an organized shopping list ready for a *fast* trip to the market -- all on one sheet. The top "Menu" portion is in calendar format and shows your family "what's cooking" that week; the bottom "Shopping List" portion helps you and your family prepare your list for those meals quickly! Includes a full year's supply -- 52 sheets -- one for each week. It helps you get organized, shop faster, save grocery money, keep the right foods in stock, and eat healthier. The brochure Eating for a Healthy Heart and to Help Prevent Cancer is enclosed as a free bonus. 52 pages, 8½x11.

Bridal Shower Journal

SPECIAL BONUS! Includes 25 thank you cards with envelopes.
Floral bouquets adorn each of the sections of this thoughtfully organized and beautifully illustrated journal that is designed to record all the wonderful bridal shower gifts and highlights of that special day. Their descriptive sentiment is a romantic reminder of a couple's love. Sturdy softcover with spiral wire binding, 22 pages (including 6 pockets), 7x10.

Our Honeymoon: A Journal of Romantic Memories

A Great Wedding or Shower Gift
This charming journal is a wonderful "extra little something" for a wedding or shower. Patterned after our popular **Vacation Getaway,** but with the look and design for a special honeymoon. Softcover (plastic spiral binding), 36 pages (incl. pockets), 5x9.

For a listing of merchants near you that carry Blue Sky Marketing Inc. Books:

☎ Call: (651) 456-5602 or (800) 444-5450

✉ Write: Blue Sky Marketing Inc., PO Box 21583-S
St. Paul, MN, 55121-1583 USA

💻 Web: www.HomeOwnersJournal.com